The History of Als   ᴜᴏᴜ

A Personal Reflection

Lindsay Purcell BA., MSc.

Copyright © Lindsay Purcell 2020

The right of Lindsay Purcell to be identified as author of this work
have been asserted by them in accordance with sections 77 and 78
of the Copyright, Designs and Patents Act 1988.

All rights of distribution, including via film, radio, television,
photomechanical reproduction, audio storage media, electronic data
storage media and the reprinting of portions of text, are reserved.

A CIP catalogue record for this title is available from the
British Library.

ISBN 978-1-5272-6973-6 (Paperback)

"Seize the moment and fly"

L Purcell 2020

Front cover, front and back page illustrations:

© Penelope Beech, 2020

Dedications

To my lovely wife and family.

To the amazing students and staff of Alsager School, present and past.

To Kevin Jones, an old primary school friend of mine, who failed the 11+ examination. From that tender age, he was denied the opportunities I received, as there was no inclusive, comprehensive education system at the time. The picture of Kevin, crying in the school yard on results day, haunts me to this day.

The Author: Lindsay Purcell

Lindsay was born in Maerdy, a small coal mining village at the head of the Rhondda Fach, South Wales in 1951. He was educated at Ferndale Grammar School from 1962-69 and the University College of Wales, Aberystwyth from 1969-1973, where he graduated with a BA (Hons) Degree in Geography and obtained a Post-Graduate Certificate in Education.

He began his teaching career at a newly built comprehensive school in Radyr, Cardiff 1973-78, before moving to Alsager Comprehensive School in September 1978, as Head of the Geography Department. He became Head of the Humanities Faculty in 1984 and completed an MSc. in Education Management at Crewe and Alsager College, 1982-85. In 1988 he was appointed Deputy Head at the school and remained in post until his retirement in August 2007. On his retirement, he continued to be employed by the Heads in Alsager, co-ordinating the work of the 'partnership' of Alsager Schools, known as the Alsager Community Trust (ACT). Three years after his retirement, he was invited onto the Board of Governors of Alsager School, as a Community Governor and in September 2017 became Chair of Governors.

Lindsay has lived all this time in Alsager, with his wife Maureen. Both his children, Gareth and Hannah, went to Alsager School where they were happy and successful. Rugby Union and skiing have been two major interests in his life. Now retired from playing rugby, he is a Trustee at Congleton Rugby Club and still tries to get in six weeks skiing each year, although the Covid pandemic put a halt to this ambition in 2020.

Acknowledgements

In writing this History of Alsager School, I have drawn on the help and support of many different people. I am so grateful to them and would like to thank them all sincerely, at the outset.

Tina and Matthew Buckingham, at Muddy Publishing Ltd, for being enormously supportive and helpful with the guidance given and for publishing the book.

Headteachers, David Black and Richard Middlebrook, for their ideas and expert knowledge, going back in time.

Headteacher, Jim Andrews, for the meticulous way in which he kept his daily headteacher's log. Also to his predecessors for their logs. These documents were invaluable sources of information.

Jane Griffiths, the school's Learning Resource Centre Manager, has been a wonderful support in so many ways, including providing IT advice, chasing down photos, old school newsletters, newspaper cuttings and networking. She has really thrown herself into the project and I couldn't have managed without her.

Penelope Beech for the creative illustrations, which adorn the front cover and first and last pages of the book. Penelope was a student at Alsager School from 1991-1998, before going on to study English at Fitzwilliam College, Cambridge. She is now a successful publisher and illustrator in London.

Ian Macpherson, for outlining, in some detail, those successful early years of comprehensive education.

Alan Hughes, a walking pal of mine and former student at the old Christ Church and Secondary Schools, for describing beautifully what life was like as a student. Alan also provided photographs of the time.

Andrea O'Neill, Liane Young and Adele Snape, for their help with curriculum and pastoral questions.

Jackie Lamprell, Mr Middlebrook's PA, for finding so many pieces of information during the period of the project.

The indomitable Pat Arnott, for chasing round the families of former students for information and photos.

Annette Owen, former Personnel Manager and Carys Dougill, former Finance Manager, for their incredible memories and information on staffing and financial affairs.

John Higgins, who taught at the school from 1962-1968. He brought me a treasure trove of archive material, much of which had been passed on to him by Rural Studies teacher Don Bury.

Sonia Cross who was a mine of information and source of photos.

Andy Pennance for his description of the halcyon days of the staff football team.

Sarah Franks for managing the book accounts.

Local historian, Jim Sutton, for advice on publishing a first book.

Many staff and former staff who provided information and hunted down photographs - including Pat Sutton, Alvan Ikoku, Wyn Jones, Steve Marshall, Roger Greaves, Shirley Cross, Pat Edwards, Val Hollins, Graham Shaw, Alison Pole, Andy Evans, Steph Wise, Vince Galley, Sue Reissing, Ashley Owen, Alison Bason. Jackie Latham, Norman Boughey, Eric Marshall, Joyce Halsall, John Lyne.

Parents from Alsager and beyond who I badgered for information and photos - including - Kath Andrews, Ray and Alan Maclean, Stuart and Liz Burkinshaw, Sue and Paul Davies, Sheila Large, Alan and Rosemary Caddy, Anne and Frank Cueto, The Mack Family, David and Carolyn Lewis, Helen Pickford, Gary Pickford, Simon Talbot, Ken Livingston, Tim Smith, Marie Atkinson, Jonathan

Broomhall, Mike and Val Broomhall, Co. Cllr. Shirley Jones, Kath Reader, Emma Sutton, Wayne Barlow.

Finally, my understanding wife Maureen, for supporting me during the writing of this book and for being ignored for five months.

This book has been written with the permission of Alsager School. The vast majority of the photographs included in the book are copyright of Alsager School and permission has been given for them to be included within the book. Permission for the publication of other photos has been granted by individual families where it has been possible to contact them. The author is eternally grateful to both Alsager School and the individual families for this kind permission.

Sponsorship

The publication of this History of Alsager School, in the form that I had intended, would never have moved beyond the planning phase, without the incredibly generous sponsorship of the following individuals, companies and organisations. They have my sincere thanks for their support, not only because it allowed me to indulge my own personal project but also because all the money raised from the sale of the book, will go to Alsager School, for the benefit of the young people who study there.

The sponsors are:

Peter Coates

Rosemary and Barry Leese and family

The B'Hoys of Alsager

The Rotary Club of Alsager

Alsager Round Table

Stephenson Browne: Independent Estate Agents

Andrew Edwards: Funeral Directors

The International Lions Club of Alsager

Alsager Ladies Circle

Mair and George Mason

Contents

Chapter One: Introduction

There was only so much gardening and walking a person could do during 'Covid lockdown', so I began to focus on a project that had been at the back of my mind for a number of years. As was often the case, life got in the way and it never got started.

I had always wanted to turn my hand to writing a book and for me there was no better subject than The History of Alsager School and the people who had studied and worked there. This book is not, by any stretch of the imagination, a definitive work and I am no Dan Snow or David Olusoga. There are sure to be some chronological and factual inaccuracies, for which I most humbly apologise at the outset.

During the period covered by this book, there have been thousands of marvellous young people through the doors of the school and hundreds of teaching and support staff. Thinking that readers would be interested in seeing names of students and staff from their past, I have included many within the pages of this book. In doing so, of course, there is always the inherent danger of upsetting those whose names do not appear.

There have been so many excellent students and staff over the years with an extraordinary array of gifts, skills, talents and character traits, worthy of mention in any book. I can only apologise now for their lack of inclusion.

These exceptional talents have meant that over the years, many individuals have gone on to lead successful and fulfilling lives. Many went on to prestigious apprenticeships in companies like Bentley, Rolls Royce, British Rail, British Aerospace, British Gas and other notable companies. Large numbers set up their own businesses locally and beyond and others learned skilled trades which were put to good use. Huge numbers went on to some of the best universities in the land and then pursued a wide range of professions or stayed on in university life.

Meeting and teaching these young people was the high point of my career at Alsager School and as I move into my 'golden years', it is always interesting to see how this huge body of potential is harnessed by our community and society in general. I hope the large majority of these young people will look back at their time at Alsager School with great fondness, and feel that it was a place where they were able to grasp the opportunities on offer and fulfil the potential inside them.

As the dialogue unfolds in these pages, it becomes impossible, at times, to separate my story of Alsager School from the constant educational change, imposed by our 'political masters' at Westminster.

The recurring debate over the 35 years I was in teaching can largely be summarised as follows:

- Segregation v Inclusion of students between schools and within schools
- The most effective method of assessment - different examinations for different abilities v one exam which fits all; continual assessment through coursework and modular units v linear courses with terminal exams
- The status of Academic and Vocational Pathways
- National or Local control of the education system
- How best to manage the scarce financial resource given to schools.

The above were ever present challenges which all schools had to come to terms with, in ways which best suited the needs of their particular school communities. They most certainly, were not the reasons for my long association with teaching in general and Alsager School in particular. Below, I have tried to list the important things which made me get out of bed in the morning, with enthusiasm (on most days!) and travel all of four minutes to school.

- The cut and thrust of banter and debate with many fantastic staff
- The energy in the staff room
- Trying to build working relationships with all students
- Teaching students who you knew were brighter than you
- Those moments of enlightenment, when students began to enjoy my subject and thought they could succeed in it
- Lovely memories of school trips and extra-curricular activities with students and staff
- Standing before a whole year group and giving assemblies.
- Observing an outstanding lesson prepared and delivered by one of my colleagues
- The close-knit relationship with partner primary schools, through Alsager Community Trust (ACT)
- Working with an experienced Governing Body which always provided wise and supportive counsel
- The rough and tumble of rugby training on a Thursday
- School productions and concerts
- Staff cricket matches
- Living a 'stone's throw' from school, for over 40 years, and never having had any bother from students
- Meeting ex-students at the pub or in the Village.

When I was Deputy Head, I had the very pleasant job of showing prospective parents around school. Without fail, as they walked around the classrooms, parents would always comment on how calm and purposeful the school environment seemed. With great pride, I always told parents that both my children went to the school and so too, did the children of Mr Andrews and Mr Black, along with the children of the majority of the staff. The school was that good. The other fact I used to mention to parents on their tour, was that if you took a dozen students out of each year group of 250, then Alsager School would be like 'Heaven on Earth'. Unfortunately, those twelve students often took up a disproportionate amount of staff time!

Finally, during my time at Alsager School, I had the immense pleasure of working with three enlightened and supportive Headteachers and hundreds of teaching and support staff colleagues, many of whom I am proud to call my friends. I have witnessed a colossal number of changes, many of which have been initiated by the school for the benefit of our students, but many have been driven by successive Governments and Education Secretaries of State, often with their own political agendas, but more of that later in the book.

I hope you enjoy my story of Alsager School and how its staff, students and external influences have impacted on the organisation you see today.

Chapter Two: Base-Line Assessment

No self-respecting sequence of lessons on a new topic would begin without the teacher doing some form of assessment of the students' existing knowledge or understanding of that topic. In my meetings with Primary Heads during my retirement years, I learned that this was 'base-line' assessment. At the end of the topic the teacher was then able to assess how much new learning had taken place.

All very technical!

To my readers this is your base-line assessment. 15 questions on the History of Alsager School and Educational Change in the UK.

1. How many Headteachers has Alsager Secondary School had from 1952 to 2020?
2. When did Alsager Secondary School become a Comprehensive School?
3. Which Secretary of State for Education created more comprehensive schools than any other?
4. How many Secretaries of State for Education have there been since Alsager School became a Comprehensive School?
5. Only 4 Secretaries of State for Education lasted into a 4th year of office. Name them.
6. In what year did Mr Black take over from Mr Andrews as Headteacher?
7. Seven teachers have taught at Alsager School for more than 35 years. Can you name 3?
8. In what year was the National Curriculum introduced?
9. Prior to the National Curriculum, what were the only two compulsory subjects on the school curriculum?
10. Which Prime Minister set out his priority for a second term of office as 'Education, Education, Education'?

11. How many OFSTED inspections has Alsager School been through?
12. In what year was the school finally awarded its 'Outstanding' grade by OFSTED?
13. How many Chairs of Governors has Alsager School had since 1955?
14. When did Alsager School become an Academy and what benefits did this change of status bring to the school?
15. What is ACT?

The answers to these questions will unfold during your reading of this history but if you are part of that generation in which 'instant gratification' holds sway, you could always go to Appendix 1 and take an early peak at the answers!

Chapter Three: The Early Years

A walk along Church Road in Alsager will take you past a picturesque building, which was really Alsager's first permanent school. Designed by renowned architect Sir George Gilbert Scott, it was opened in 1848. Other buildings designed by Sir George include the Midland Grand Hotel at St Pancras Station, St John's College Chapel, Cambridge University and Sandbach School. Sir George's grandson, Giles, designed the Anglican Cathedral in Liverpool. So no expense was spared on Alsager's first permanent school. It's a shame the creative architectural design skills of the Gilbert Scott family did not extend to our current buildings which are rather more functional than 'picturesque'.

"Of course, the old Church School is now a private dwelling, adjacent to a small residential development, recently built to a design, extremely sympathetic to the late eighteenth century style of the old school building. Prior to this, the school began life as a Charity School, funded by the Misses Alsager and housed in what became the Christ Church Parsonage. For over a century this was the sole source of education for the children of the village's pauper and working classes. It started with around 20 pupils but by 1848 had over 200. In 1900 it became a secondary school only, as a Church of England infant and primary school was built off Sandbach Road North. This building now houses the infant department of Highfields Primary School. Prior to 1900, a small fee (pennies only) was expected from parents who could afford it; the children of paupers were paid for. School records show that there was a great deal of concern over bad language and behaviour among pupils - a birch tree in the headmaster's garden was nicknamed the 'tree of knowledge', as it provided sticks with which to punish pupils who misbehaved. There also appears to have been fairly frequent school closures because of epidemics of measles, diphtheria etc. and much absenteeism at harvest time".

Extract from 'Alsager: The Place and Its People' ED. J.C.Sutton.

In 1952, the Headteacher was John O. Hughes. There were 8 teaching staff, 3 dinner ladies and 118 pupils, including my walking pal, Alan Hughes who provided this early insight into what the school was like, along with some photographs.

"As well as the main school building, the school also made use of the old Vicarage, which was at the end of the drive, up past the current church hall. Mr Hughes had his office in what was the vicar's study. It was usual practice, for staff in the main school to send a pupil to warn Mr Hughes of the approach of important visitors. The pupil could run through the shrubbery, over a ha-ha, into the garden and round to the Head's study, more swiftly than the visitor's car could drive round via Hassall Road."

(These buildings were still being used by the school when I joined in 1978 but neither the Vicarage nor the Old School were popular with the caretaking staff, as they were thought to be haunted. The ghost stories they used to tell at the time were very popular with our students!)

"The school had only four classes, one for each year. The curriculum included Maths, English, History, Geography and Music for all; Woodwork and Technical Drawing (for the boys) and Domestic Science (for the girls). The DS was actually taught in a bungalow where the church hall currently stands. There were separate playgrounds for the boys and girls and corporal punishment was still often used by the Headteacher.

World War Two led to a huge increase in Alsager's population, as munitions workers moved with their families from Woolwich to take up jobs at the new armaments factory at Radway Green. The school was bursting at the seams. Plans were drawn up and a new, larger school was built on land behind the old school, fronting onto Hassall Road.

In 1955 the old school closed its doors, at the end of the Spring Term, just as the pupils started their Easter Holidays. The new Alsager Secondary School opened on the Hassall Road site, at the start of the Summer Term 1955. It was suddenly a larger school, absorbing the older pupils from the surrounding areas, including Barthomley, Smallwood, Rode Heath, Scholar Green and Mow Cop. Children aged 11+ were bussed in to Alsager, from these areas. From many of these schools, staff transferred, to work alongside the existing teachers at Alsager School, increasing the staff number to 15. The outlying schools then became primary schools."

Significantly, there was also a new Headteacher - Mr Austin J. Hawkes. Mr Hughes remained as joint deputy head, along with Miss Win Holmes, until his retirement.

Mr Hawkes' first remarks in the Headteacher's log book are:

"On this day 21st April 1955, the teaching staff, secretary, caretaker and I contrived to open the new Alsager Secondary School in good order. Attendance was 252".

Alsager Secondary School (in the Old Church School Buildings) circa 1954.

Margaret Bebbington was a teacher at the school, at this time of significant change. She writes:

"It took some time for the children from the outlying schools to settle down in their new surroundings. The atmosphere in small village schools had been very different to that of this much larger

21

establishment, with many specialist rooms and long corridors. The pupils were no longer taught in form groups with one form teacher but moved from one subject to another. Apart from the emotional upheaval, the physical toll on the younger children was immense".

The teaching block was today's Parker Building and the staff room is now Mr Middlebrook's study. The pupils in the first top class (Year 4) were all made prefects, to help with the discipline of the larger number of pupils.

Alan Hughes continues his description as follows:

"By the standards of the day, the new school had everything, including a range of classrooms, a school hall, a gym and a dining hall. However the latter was never big enough and lunch had to be in two sittings.

Alsager Tennis Club had recently vacated its courts by the Grig woodland, to move to new courts in the village, which meant these were now available to the pupils at lunchtime, so tennis became a popular sport in the school.

Alsager Secondary School Staff and Prefects 1956 including (backrow left to right) Miss Winifred Holmes, Deputy Head, 3rd, John Hughes, former Head, 5th, Austin Hawkes, Headmaster, 7th.

The curriculum was also extended to include Science, Metalwork and PE, with ballroom dancing lessons on offer at lunchtimes. Those older boys who joined this club got a very pleasant surprise some

22

School Dinners in the Old Canteen 1959 (just through from today's reception area).

months later, when they were invited to join the Alsager College Ballroom Dancing classes on a Monday evening, as there was a distinct lack of male partners. Lucky them! Other extra-curricular options at the time were photography, cricket, hockey and football."

So the story goes, not long after he had taken up his headship, Austin J Hawkes was familiarising himself with the local area, when he came across Alsager Mere. There he saw a pair of swans in all their glory. This gave him the idea for a new school badge and the swan remains the centre piece of our badge to this day. Well done Mr Hawkes!

As far as I can detect, PE was not formally added to the curriculum until 1955 and neither is RE mentioned. Under the very significant, 1944 Butler Education Act, the only two compulsory subjects in the curriculum were PE and RE. In other words those subjects responsible for the spiritual and physical well-being of young people were not being taught. I find this hard to believe and await information to the contrary!

Another significant fact about secondary education in Alsager at this time and indeed until 1971, was that Alsager Secondary School was a 'secondary modern school'. Nationally, at the age of 11, all young people had to sit the 11+ exam, a test designed to differentiate by ability. In Alsager, the boys who passed the 11+ travelled to either Crewe or Sandbach Grammar Schools, the girls to Crewe or Congleton Grammar Schools. Those who failed the 11+ stayed in Alsager.

On 1st September 1959, Mr Frederick G. Parker took over as Headteacher from Austin Hawkes. On this day in the school log book he writes

"Reverend Lewis came to welcome me. The school is in good heart and began well."

Alsager Secondary School Cricket Team circa 1956.

During this period the curriculum in Years 1 and 2 offered a broad general education, with year one being referred to as 'Reception' and Year 2 as 'Remove'. The curriculum in Years 3 and 4 was more specialised and based on Cheshire's 'Alternative Courses', comprising five broad optional areas - Technical (Boys); Technical (Girls); Commerce; Rural Studies; Practical. More specifically, subjects offered were English, Maths, History, Geography, Science, Music, Woodwork, Metalwork, Technical Drawing, Cookery, Needlework, Typing, Rural Studies, Art and PE. There was a certain amount of mixed ability teaching but English and Maths were streamed, according to ability. More able students tended to be directed into the Technical Courses.

Open Day exhibits in the Gym 1959.

Rural Studies was still on the curriculum until the late 1970's. It was affectionately known by the pupils as 'double digging', as it was spread over two lessons. The reason I mention this, is that at the end of my first week in post, last two periods on the Friday afternoon, I had to cover for the legendary Don Bury, who was off school ill. This was a really fun experience for the new boy on the block! At that time the school had a wonderful allotment, garden, greenhouses, a poultry shed and, for a time, even kept four St Kilda sheep and 'Penelope' the pig. The animals were kept overnight in the shed, (now the PE athletics store) half way down the back drive. Sadly they kept escaping, so eventually had to go!

Don Bury's Rural Studies Group hard at work.

Penelope the pig.

No external examinations, such as CSEs or O Levels were taken until a few pupils stayed on at school, on a voluntary basis, to take CSE in the mid-1960s. This followed the Newsom Report which recommended that the school leaving age be raised to 16. The Act of Parliament which followed, known as ROSLA (Raising of the School Leaving Age) meant that schools like Alsager were now able to offer external examinations to all pupils at the beginning of the 1970s.

ROSLA, itself, was an interesting time. It sent waves of fear across the teaching profession, about what it was going to do with this cohort of young people, who were being made to stay on at school, against their will for the most part, for an additional year. However, after a short period of adjustment, schools, including Alsager, seemed to settle into the 'new norm' quite quickly.

Education was very different in those days, not only in terms of the curriculum on offer and the fact that selection took place at the tender age of 11 years, but also from the point of view that corporal punishment was widely used in schools across the country. Mr Parker documents in his log an occasion when he had to speak to an over-zealous teacher about this very issue:

"I spoke to a teacher who lightly caned a second year girl, using an unauthorised form of cane. I spoke about this and explained that I did not want children caned without my permission and that punishment of girls must be carried out by the Senior Mistress or an alternative punishment awarded".

Alsager Secondary School Staff during the first year of Headteacher Mr Frederick Parker, 1959.

On May 3rd 1960, one of the longest serving members of Alsager School was appointed by Mr Parker and his Governors. He went on to be associated with the school as teacher and Governor for almost 50 years. He will best be remembered as a much loved Head of Year. It was of course, Mr Mike Elkin. On that day Mr Parker comments as follows about Mike's appointment:

"Interview of Mr Michael Elkin for the post of assistant teacher of general subjects and work with backward juniors"

In these days of political correctness, it is difficult to comprehend the terminology used to describe some of our young people in the 1960's. This is another example of the differences between education then and now, and how things have developed and improved exponentially.

A very young Mr Elkin with his Senior Football Team 1961-62.

On July 7th 1960, Alsager Secondary School entertained the mighty Crewe Grammar School in a cricket match, to celebrate the opening of its new cricket square. Our boys were victorious by two wickets. In terms of success in sport, Alsager School never looked back.

At the start of the Autumn Term in 1966, there were 111 pupils in the first year and 483 pupils on roll in total. Remember, young people still left school at the age of 15 years but they did have the option to stay on for that extra year. This particular year, only 11 pupils chose to stay on into Year 5, mainly due to the fact that Crewe Technical College offered attractive new practical courses.

Miss Barbara Mason (the future Mrs Graham Harvey) and Head, Mr Frederick Parker with the Girl's Hockey team 1961-62.

At the end of 1966, Deputy Head Miss Win Holmes retired and Mr John King took over in that role. From my research into Miss Holmes, people told me

The Hollinshead Hall under construction 1963.

"She may have been small in stature but could she pack a punch!" Figuratively speaking, of course!

Many of the entries in the Headteachers' Log Books relate to appointments, staff absences, accidents, trips out of school and other daily occurrences of this nature. I could not let the reason pass, for Mrs Mair Mason's absence on November 27th 1967.

"Mrs Mason absent due to the outbreak of foot and mouth disease on her husband's farm. Parents of five children notified me that they were being kept off school for this reason too. The situation is grave".

Not exactly a Coronavirus pandemic but even in the 60's we were not immune from these sorts of events!

Mrs Mason was one of quite a strong contingent of Welsh staff at Alsager Comprehensive School, who were there when I joined the school in 1978. They included Mrs Mair Needham, Head of Year, Mr Medwyn Jones, Head of PE and Mr Wyn Jones, Head of Maths, all of whom made me feel very much at home, from day one.

Mr Parker retired as Headteacher on August 31st 1968. His last comments were about the encouraging CSE results that year and how the staff entertained him at the White Lion at Weston.

He writes:

"This is my last entry as Headmaster of the school. It is made with a heavy heart, after nine years of happiness. The school has grown up into a very happy family. I wish it every success in the future. I am grateful to my staff and governors and especially to the children for making my task an easy one.... I have been proud to serve you".

I would concur with Mr Parker. Although the school became much bigger in subsequent years, it always remained 'a very happy family'. A place you want to send your children to be educated and a place in which you would want to teach.

In September 1968 Mr John King, took over as acting Headteacher until 5th January 1970, when Mr Jim Andrews arrived as the new Head.

Mrs Mair Needham, Senior Tutor, my surrogate mother at Alsager, and Alderman John Hollinshead, Chair of Governors. Circa 1975.

Chapter 4:   A new Era of Comprehensive Education

Mr Andrews' brief was to expand and develop Alsager Secondary School into Alsager Comprehensive School. To create a single, much larger, school which would accommodate all the young people in Alsager, from the ages of 11-18 years, mixed both socially and academically. Hopefully, an exciting and achievable challenge! Jim Andrews had come straight from the British Virgin Islands, where he had been Director of Education, similarly tasked with setting up comprehensive education on those islands.

Alsager Comprehensive opened on 7th September 1971. The New Block, now the Andrews Building, was ready and there were 220 pupils in the new first year intake. Ian White, a former Chair of Governors, started school that day and reminisced:

"We were a privileged group with new text books and facilities and although there were fewer buildings - no Leisure Centre, Music Block, Science Block or Design Centre- we had the newly completed Andrews Building (for over 20 years, simply the New Block) and so there was plenty of scope for the new first years to get lost".

Alsager School Teaching Staff circa 1972.

Alsager was one of the first schools in Cheshire to gain 'comprehensive' status. Surprisingly, to many people, given her later antithesis to the comprehensive ideal, Margaret Thatcher was Minister for Education and under her stewardship, more schools became comprehensive than at any other time.

During the early 1970s the school grew from the previous, small, secondary modern of around 550 pupils to a very large, comprehensive school. September 1978 witnessed its largest intake, with 340 students, 13 form entry and an overall student roll of 1700, with 94 teaching staff. The school was most certainly overcrowded and had to resort to bringing the old Church School building back into commission, as an Annexe.

One evening in the mid-seventies, disaster struck in the middle of a governors' meeting. Smoke began to appear from one of the Science laboratories and the governors had to abandon the meeting, evacuate the building and watch the science block go up in flames. The water from the fire engines filled 'the well' which was a feature of the old Social Area, the area where our newest Science labs are today. This was a major disruption to that period of expansion.

According to Ian Macpherson, one of the Deputy Heads during that period of great expansion, four key elements came together to allow the school to thrive and, very quickly, enhance its reputation.

Firstly, the appointment of well qualified, young staff, able to complement the well-established and loyal teachers who were already at the school.

Secondly, an intake which comprised the whole ability range of young people from Alsager and the surrounding settlements, which in turn presented the school with the opportunity to develop a large, academic Sixth Form.

Thirdly, the development of an appropriate breadth of experience for all students, including a broad and balanced curriculum.

SMT and Faculty Heads and Senior Tutors 1980.

Finally, appropriate (if not architecturally state of the art) accommodation was provide by Cheshire County Council, to house over 1500 students, in those first few years. This included Alsager Leisure Centre, which was handed over on August 20th 1975 and officially opened by the British Olympic athlete, Derek Ibbotson, on 3rd January 1977. It has provided the school with first rate sporting facilities ever since.

Initially there was an understandable degree of scepticism from some parents, who were concerned that their children were being denied a place at a grammar school. It is worth noting that some of these concerns were from parents whose children realistically, would not have passed the 11+. Unquestionably, the pressure was on Jim Andrews. He and the school had to succeed! At an early meeting with new parents in a packed hall, Mr Andrews set out some very ambitious expectations, for the number of students who would gain 5+ GCE 'O' Level passes. There was some doubt in the community but in the event, his forecast had been on the cautious side and his comprehensive students exceeded his expectations and vindicated the concept of education for all Alsager's young people in the same school. In the subsequent years, GCE 'A' Levels came on stream and from the very start Alsager students gained places at some of Britain's top universities, including Oxford and Cambridge.

Mr Andrews writes on the first week of the Spring Term, January 1989

"During this first week of term we have received seven offers from Cambridge and one from Oxford".

On May 7th 1992 the school was visited by the 'Independent' newspaper, so that it could be included in their annual 'Good Schools Guide'. In September 1992, the school featured in both the Independent and Sunday Times survey of top comprehensive schools nationally. Indeed, in the Sunday Times we made the top 25 for A Level. Amazing! This level of success in external exams has continued through to today's students and has always been an achievement, of which the school is proud.

Staff photograph 1990.

It is important to stress that all pupils were encouraged to succeed and follow their own career pathways, given their interests, aptitudes and abilities. For example, in the 1970/80s there were a good many opportunities for prestigious apprenticeships locally. Royal Ordnance, Rolls Royce and British Rail were on the doorstep and many of our students went to train at these companies. I was fortunate to attend the Royal Ordnance presentation events for many years and on these occasions it was common for former Alsager students to receive apprentice of the year awards, for their particular years or even overall apprentice of the year, in the face of fierce competition.

Alongside this drive for high standards and achievement in the classroom, the school also put a great deal of emphasis, and still does, on the extra-curricular side of school life. When I first arrived at the school in September 1978, I was astonished by the number of activities on offer, not just the range of sports but also the emphasis on outdoor pursuits. My life had always been dominated by rugby, so it gave me a chance to broaden my horizons. Some staff at Alsager, in those days, used to take their forms away camping at weekends and there were always sailing, canoeing and climbing weekends. The Design-Technology courtyard could be full of sailing dinghies and canoes, when they were not in use and there was a big store room full of tents and other camping and climbing equipment. Mr Andrews, himself, was into outdoor pursuits and encouraged staff and students to get involved wherever they could. A favourite question of his at interview was 'what will you offer the school outside of the classroom?' It was an expectation, not an option.

In many respects, education in the 1970's and right up to 1988, was a different world. Most teachers still worked long hours, preparing lessons and marking. The pressure to encourage students to succeed was always present at Alsager. However, the obsession with 'data collection', sophisticated assessment arrangements, student tracking systems and other complex administrative procedures were largely absent. In essence, teachers had a little more time for the extra-curricular side of life and out-of-classroom experiences! For instance, in those days, staff outside the PE department, were always ready to coach school teams. The school pitches then were in excellent condition, as we had our own, full-time groundsman, Reg.

PE Department circa 1977, with additional staff who ran teams, together with Reg, the groundsman.

I was appointed Deputy Head in September 1988, taking over from the formidable Mrs Sheila Riley. I spent a rather nervous summer break worrying about one thing in particular, the fact that I would have to lead large groups of students in assemblies, on a regular basis. I bought a number of books on 'Secondary School Assembly Themes' but in the event, I hardly used them. Topical newspaper articles and experiences from my youth proved to be far more fertile fields of interest. All linked to the Christian message, of course, for in those days the majority of school assemblies (51%) had to be of a Christian nature and school assembly themes had to be recorded. I quickly got into the routine of delivering assemblies and they became a favourite part of my role. One year I made the mistake of giving the same assembly twice to a particular year group. Unfortunately, Mrs Sue Jones (Technology) and Mr Steve Marshall (P.E.) were in the Hall and they never let me forget the transgression, until I retired. Perhaps I should have focused to a greater extent on the Christian principle of forgiveness!

Lindsay Purcell and Mike Elkin leading an assembly.

The end of the eighties and the start of the nineties, were times of great change, not just at Alsager School, not just in education, but in the world as a whole and some of these changes were reflected in Mr Andrews' log.

For instance on November 11th 1989 he wrote:

"Alsager School held its Annual PTA Craft Fair, Derek Pedley and Mark Sherwood won the English Schools' Life Saving Championships and the Berlin Wall fell".

The rich tapestry of life, all in one day!

A major change for the school took place on January 24th 1990 when the decision was made, after much debate, to move to a 25 period week - 5 one hour lessons per day. Great concern was expressed by the Design, PE and Science faculties that this would not be enough time for practical subjects. Over time, things worked out well and eventually the school moved to a 50-period fortnightly timetable, which allowed greater curriculum and timetable flexibility.

On January 17ᵗʰ 1991 Mr Andrews wrote with some poignancy:

"Hostilities commenced in the Gulf War today. Some of our former pupils are there. Our thoughts go with them".

October 30ᵗʰ was a much better day for the school as it saw the opening of the synthetic astro turf pitch by Olympian, Martin Grimley. Anne Winterton MP was also in attendance.

The astro turf being constructed.

The funds for this pitch were raised by Cheshire County Council selling off the school's two grass hockey pitches on Dunnocksfold Road, where the Hellyar-Brook Estate is today. Eventually, the school received just over £1 million from the LA for the project, with an additional contribution from Congleton Borough. The astro turf was one of the first in Cheshire but the process of laying it did not go smoothly. For a while local residents, and subsequently the press, referred to it as the building of a 'new stalag'. The school also had to work hard to draw down the funds from the LA and the Borough and half way through the laying of the synthetic turf, the contractors went to a wedding in Ireland and forgot to return! They were eventually tracked down and turned up a month late. Further health and safety problems with the floodlights in high winds, caused more delays but we got there in the end. The facility has proved an enormous benefit to the school and community over many years.

Also in 1991 the Alsager School Trust was born. This was a covenanting scheme, whereby parents and friends of the school, gifted a sum of money, usually each month, to provide 'education extras', to enrich the curriculum for our young people. These extras were the resources which the main education budget was unable to afford. As the Trust had charitable status, it could claim back tax from HMRC, provided people giving the donations paid income tax.

Mr Ian Macpherson, when he was Head at Holmfirth High School, started a similar scheme and I benefited from his experience, before starting the Alsager Trust. Between 1991 and 2020 the Trust raised £416,000 and paid for an exciting range of resources, from which students benefited greatly. It also donated two considerable sums to support the Jill Bristow Performing Arts Centre and the recently refurbished tennis courts. The Trust still exists today, as the Parents in Partnership (PiP) fund. A much more appropriate name and long may parents and friends of the school continue to contribute. For much of the time the fund has been in existence, it has been very well managed by Alison Bason and the school is most grateful to her.

On 3rd March 1992, Princess Anne, the Princess Royal, visited Alsager. Young people from all Alsager Schools were invited to the Civic Centre to meet the Princess and sing a specially composed anthem called 'To Africa with Love'. The Princess had become aware of a project, initiated by Crewe and Alsager College Lecturer, Roy Pitcher, to provide fresh water wells for villages in Africa. The people of Alsager and Sandbach had raised thousands of pounds by collecting small donations for the wells. So impressed was the Princess by the project, that she requested a visit to Alsager and Sandbach to meet some of the people involved, including the young people.

The Princess Royal being introduced to members of Alsager School Choir.

Co. Cllr. Shirley Jones was so delighted with the singing that day, that she requested the Alsager School Choir to sing the same anthem at her 'Civic Service' a few months later, when she was inaugurated as Mayor of Congleton Borough.

At some point in 1992, discussions took place between Mr Andrews, the three Deputies - Messrs Clarke, Austen and Purcell - and the school Governors, about the merits of changing the school name, from Alsager Comprehensive School, to simply Alsager School. The precise reasons for such a change seem to be lost in the mist of time. Most unusually, there is no record of the change in Mr Andrew's daily log, and governor minutes from those days were all in paper form and have long since been destroyed. I can only put forward the following theory based on my recollections of the time.

The 1988 Education Reform Act put schools firmly in the 'market place', as will be explained later. Throughout the country, City Technology Colleges were springing up and an increasing number of Local Authority schools were opting out of LA control to become Grant Maintained schools. There were considerable financial incentives for schools to do this, in the early days. Although Cheshire held fast, with only two secondary schools breaking ranks and going their own way, competition was building amongst schools. National league tables did not help in this respect. Other local schools began to drop the word 'comprehensive' from their names and so Alsager School, seemed a more appropriate name for the climate in which we were operating. To this day, the only school in Cheshire East, to keep the word 'comprehensive' within its school name, as far as I am aware, is Holmes Chapel.

I can only smile at the fact that Jim Andrews, that most precise keeper of the school log, makes no mention of the school name change. For me, that's an indication of Jim, deep down, remaining true to his comprehensive principles and not being altogether in favour of the change. Pragmatism seems to have won the day!

Jim Andrews in his office.

The name Alsager School, does however have a certain appeal and link to its community and I am so glad that it has remained to this day, even though there have been a number of changes to the status of the school in subsequent years, most notably when it became a Multi-Academy Trust in September 2013.

Alsager School
An Achieving School - A Caring Community

School logo.

It was also around this time that the issue of drugs began to raise its head as an issue for schools around the country and Alsager School was not immune. On September 22nd 1992, the school held its first 'drugs forum' for parents. I have never seen the Hollinshead Hall so full. Every seat was taken and parents were standing at the rear and sides of the auditorium. Representatives from Cheshire County Council and Cheshire Police's Drug Unit gave a first rate, interactive presentation, in which they informed parents of the stark realities of recreational drugs use amongst young people, within the communities of Cheshire. The evening backed up Jim Andrew's age-old mantra to parents, at school presentation evenings *"Do you know where your children are and what they are doing?"* This evening was followed by other drugs awareness workshops, aimed at smaller groups of parents, where different substances were passed around and discussed but not sampled, of course!

As a school, the Governors have always taken a zero tolerance approach to young people bringing drugs into school. Rightly, they have felt that they have a prime duty to safeguard all the other students in their care and that these students should not be put at risk. Interestingly, on the rare occasions when drugs were brought into school, it was often the students themselves or parents, who made us first aware of the person/persons bringing them into

43

school. It's as if there is an in-built, self-regulatory system at work. Young people, for the most part, know what is right and wrong and students who bring drugs into school cross that 'invisible line'.

On December 9th 1993, Mrs Hazel Ash, our fantastic school cook of 28 years, retired. Her contribution went well beyond her role as cook and she was a much loved and respected member of staff who was greatly missed.

On 24th March 1993 Mr Andrews wrote one of his most significant entries into his log.

"Today David Black was appointed as the new Head of Alsager School".

Mr Andrews had already announced to Governors, his intent to retire on 23rd July 1993.

On the evening of 23rd July, a huge reception and supper was held, at the Alsager site of Crewe and Alsager College, at which so many past and present staff were in attendance to say their farewells to a very highly respected headmaster. During the evening, amongst the speeches, a letter of congratulations from Nat Lofthouse, the former Bolton Wanderers and England Centre Forward and boyhood hero of Jim, was read out. Jim was a 'Bolton lad!'

Mr Andrews signed off as follows, after almost 23 years at the helm:

"Today I left Alsager School. I was given a right royal farewell; everyone was so kind and generous. It has been a privilege to be Head of Alsager School".

Throughout much of Jim's time at the helm, I had the privilege to work alongside Deputy Heads Philip Clarke and Hedley Austen. Between us, we accumulated 63 years, as Deputies to both Jim Andrews and David Black. Philip was the longest serving with 26 years, then myself with 19 years, closely followed by Hedley with 18. The other Deputies in Jim Andrews' time were John King, Sheila Riley, Ian Macpherson and Jim Edwards.

Students Present Mr Andrews with a retirement gift in the Hollinshead Hall July 1993.

Jim Andrews at his retirement party with his Deputy Heads, Philip Clarke, Hedley Austen and Lindsay Purcell.

Chapter Five: Extraordinary Talent

In researching the story of Alsager School, reading Mr Andrew's daily log was not only a real privilege, but also a very useful source of information. To him, recording the considerable achievements of a great many young people was much more important than fairly mundane daily events.

In the years following Mr Andrew's retirement, when Mr Black took over the helm and then Mr Middlebrook, it no longer was a legal requirement for heads to keep log books. Consequently, the school newsletters like 'Headlines', 'School Matters', PINC and SPIRIT became important sources of historical information, on the achievements of the school generally and its students in particular. Some of the achievements of Alsager's talented young people appear below but there are so many other students whose achievements were of equal worth and could have been included within these pages.

Alsager School Archery Team who were English Schools' Champions for 3 years. Gordon Citrine and Sylvia Harris pictured, were individual national champions.

Alsager Company of Archers was established at the school in 1974 and from 1977-1979, Alsager Comprehensive School became English Schools Archery Champions. The teams were led by Sylvia Harris and Gordon Citrine, both of whom went on to be individual champions in their age groups. Richard Wales, my boss at the time, was the member of staff and driving force behind these outstanding achievements.

First school rugby team, with Anthony Whittaker, captain, Lindsay Purcell, coach, Gary Turner student coach, Mr Jim Andrews Head and Mr Medwyn Jones, Head of PE.

January 1979. Mr Andrews wrote:

"This term, Mr Purcell started extra-curricular rugby at the school. The intention is to play competitive fixtures against other local schools".

As a Welshman, it would be remiss of me not to comment a little further on Mr Andrews' statement. Extra-curricular, competitive rugby continued at the school for the 29 years, I taught there. This would not have been possible without the support of Mr Steve Marshall. We were like Warren Gatland and Shaun Edwards, inseparable on a Thursday evening after school, during the rough and tumble of training sessions. The lads seemed to get larger, as the years went by, and the hits got harder. I never knew what parents were feeding them? The first ever captain of an Alsager rugby team was Anthony Whittaker and he can be seen holding the ball in the photograph.

We had our victories over the years but football was always the boys' main winter team sport, in which the school excelled. However, I am proud to say, a good many of our boys went on to play for Cheshire or Staffordshire and of course Mark Cueto (who played in our Sixth Form team) went on to represent England at senior level. The main outcome for Steve and me was for the lads to have fun. I am delighted to see that rugby has re-appeared as an extra-curricular option in recent years and even more delighted to see that there is now a girls' rugby team.

May 7th 1981. The U16 mixed Badminton team became Northern Champions. They played in the national final at Wellingborough on May 16th but unfortunately, that one got away!

On Thursday 20th January 1983, The Sentinel wrote an article on the developing careers of Alsager's extraordinary Sporting Twins, Deborah and Amanda Ford. Born with just one hour separating them and following similar sporting pathways, Debbie and Amanda excelled in everything. They played hockey and badminton for Cheshire

Debbie and Amanda Ford, Cheshire County Cross-Country Championships circa 1981.

48

and also ran cross-country for the County. They helped the Alsager School Badminton and Cross-country teams get to the National Schools' Finals and Debbie played hockey for Northern Counties. Superb achievements, superb athletes! Many of you will realise that Debbie then went on to teach art at Alsager School for many years.

Alsager School Cross-Country Team with Geoff Heath - Cheshire County Champions circa 1983. Geoff Heath, front row, 2nd from left.

Another superb athlete at the same time was Geoff Heath who had twice won the Cheshire Schools' Cross-Country Championships by

1982 and was going for his hat-trick. He was also Cheshire 1,500 metres champion. Geoff's older brother David also ran for Cheshire at Cross-Country and was the Air Training Corps National Cross-Country Champion. The family love of the sport did not end there, for younger sister Julie also ran for Cheshire to make it a real 'family affair!'

In 1988 Ashlyn Stevenson played in goal for the England U16 football team. To date he is the only Alsager School student to play for England at football. A coach load of supporters from school went to Wembley to watch him play. Ashlyn played youth team football for Crewe Alexandra and signed professionally for them.

Anthony Douglas, Rachel Mack and Ashlyn Stephenson.

At this same time, Rachel Mack (McCarthy) represented Cheshire and England Schools Netball at U16 level. Following Rachel's inclusion in the national team at the age of 15, it went on to win five consecutive games, including British Universities and British Colleges Under-21s. In 1991, Rachel went on to tour the Cook Islands with North West Regions (now Manchester Thunder). The team was undefeated until New Zealand sent over a team of their international players and even then, I understand, they only lost out in the last few minutes to some 'dodgy' decisions by the New Zealand umpire. Mrs Mack was not impressed! Rachel was player of the tour.

Ms Sonia Cross, then Head of PE, recounted to me the pride she felt when she and a coach full of Alsager students went to support Rachel in her first international match.

Rachel Mack England Schools U16 Netball.

"Although a super star by the time she reached Years 10 and 11, Rachel's story was one of perseverance and gradual development. In Year 7 she was selected for the school 'B' team initially but worked diligently throughout the year until she had made the 'A' team by the end of the season. From there she never looked back as her confidence and work ethic transformed her ability. Rachel was a role model for all who followed in her footsteps".

In 1989, the school entered an exceptionally talented mixed team into the National Heinz Marathon. The squad were from our cross-country team, many of whom went on to represent Cheshire and attend National trials. The team comprised twelve athletes, each of whom had to run 800m, in sequence, over the twenty six mile course. Over 30 schools competed in the North of England section of the competition. The team ran incredibly well and gained second place, six seconds behind the Liverpool Bluecoat School. Our prize was £500, a considerable amount of money back in the day. One member of the marathon squad was Rebecca Broad, another excellent all-round sportsperson. She represented Cheshire in the hurdles and attended English Schools trials.

Heinz Marathon Squad.

On February 18th 1990 the Table Tennis team won the Northern Schools Championships, under the guidance of Deputy Head, Philip Clarke. They then progressed to the Dunlop National Schools Table Tennis Finals for the first time, in which they came third. The team comprised Paul Pickford, Simon Edbury, Gary Pickford and Ben Seel. Gary had been Cheshire U16 Champion in 1989 and Ben, Cheshire's U19 Champion, while Philippa Clarke was the girl's Cheshire U13 Champion.

Alsager School Table Tennis Team, National Finalists 1990.

Philip Clarke's Alsager team certainly had a grip on Cheshire table tennis for a good many years.

Gary Pickford was an impressive all round sports person who also excelled in cricket and golf. While a 17 year old at Alsager School, he toured Australia, playing representative cricket with the best junior cricketers from Cheshire and Staffordshire, many of whom went on to play County and International cricket professionally.

In September 1990 a young man by the name of Dean Field started school. He was the first of a number of students who went on to excel in Martial Arts, others are mentioned later in this chapter. Dean became a real master of the art of Shotokan Karate and is a 'fourth dan' black belt. He first competed for England and Great Britain in 1999 and went on to win many major titles at senior level. He has been ranked as high as first in the UK, third in Europe and fifth in the world. Who knows what he could have achieved, had he not been plagued with serious injuries at the height of his career. What we do know is that as a 29 year old, he made a spectacular return from injury, to win a gold medal at the European Shotokan Karate Championships in London and is now a prominent UK coach.

1990 was also the year that Rebecca Mottershaw was included in the England Schools U16 Netball squad.

Year 8 Netball Team 1990.

If ever there was a day that summed up sporting excellence at the school, October 12th 1991, encapsulated it perfectly. Jim Andrews writes:

"The archery team won the English Schools title again. Derek Pedley and Mark Sherwood won the North West Life Saving Championships, the Girls U19 Netball Team won the Cheshire Championships and Rebecca Morgan, representing our sailing club, won the Ladies Helm at the Tatton Regatta".

July 10th 1992,

"Rebecca Lewis became the England Junior Girls, Long Jump Champion at Hull".

Rebecca Lewis in the winning Cambridge Boat at the Varsity Boat Race 1999.

This one line in Mr Andrew's log does not really represent the significance of Rebecca's achievements as an Alsager School student. The PE Department of the day regarded Rebecca as the most talented all round sports person ever to grace Alsager School. In her senior years at school, she went on to become the English Senior Girls Long Jump Champion and represented Great Britain in the Heptathlon and Long Jump. Although athletics was Rebecca's first love, she was an U18 Cheshire and North of England squad hockey player and could have played at a high level in other school sports. Many of her school athletics records still stand.

Rebecca was also an extremely conscientious and gifted student across all her subjects and secured a place at Fitzwilliam College

Cambridge, to read Natural Sciences. PE was one of her four A Level subjects and in this her mark was one of the top 5 nationally, out of an entry of 6745 students.

As you can imagine, while at Fitzwilliam, Rebecca continued to participate in a whole range of sports. She has 3 Cambridge 'Blues' for athletics. A Blue is the award a person receives when they represent Cambridge against Oxford, in an individual sporting discipline. During the three years Rebecca competed in these Athletics Varsity Matches, she won the following titles and holds the all-time record for the number of events won.

- 100m in 1997 and 99
- 200m in 98
- 100m hurdles in 97
- long jump 97 and 98
- shot 97 and 99
- javelin 97 and 98.

In 1999, her final year, Rebecca was selected for the Ladies Boat in the Varsity Boat Race, picking up her 4th 'Blue' and beating Oxford in a record time. Remarkable achievements! No wonder the PE Department regarded her as the most talented, all round sports person to come through the doors of Alsager School.

Andrew Lewis, after the Varsity football match, with his winning medal.

Rebecca, however, was not the only talented member of the Lewis family. Her older brother Andrew, another gifted all rounder, studied at Fitzwilliam College and was a Cambridge Blue in football. Simon, the youngest member of the family, who had a different skill set, including a lovely, dry sense of humour, studied at Harper Adams University and became a very successful farmer, running the family farm.

On top of these achievements, Rebecca also came to me one day, with the best request I ever received for having the afternoon off school. The Queen was coming to tea at her farm, which was on Duchy land. How could I refuse?

Summer Term 1993, Ceri Jones, Year 11, won the Royal Mail National Letter Writing Competition, out of 300,000 entries. She won £500 and over £1000's worth of computer equipment for school. She and her family had a fantastic two days in London, where Ceri was presented with her award by BBC news presenter Martin Lewis.

Ceri Jones, Royal Mail, Young Letter Writer of the Year with Martin Lewis, Newsreader 1993.

October 2nd 1993. The school's Year 8 swimming team won both the freestyle and medley relays in the National English Schools' Swimming Finals at Leicester. In the winning team were John Edgell, Simon Dennison, Eamonn Rabie and David Hyde. The Year 11 team finished 6th and 7th respectively and included Jake McCombe, Robert Edgell, Paul Bailey and Mark Hollins. Outstanding achievements all round.

19th March 1994. Year 7-10 football teams were all in the South Cheshire finals. All won apart from Year 10 who drew and had to replay.

Lee Bell joined the school in 1994 from Highfields Primary and throughout his time at school proved himself as a most promising footballer, always committed to school teams. He represented Cheshire and was a Crewe Alexandra Academy Player. When he left school in 1999 he signed professional terms with 'The Alex' and had two periods with them during his professional career, including a time as captain. He also played for Mansfield, Macclesfield Town and Burton Albion. Today, Lee is back at Crewe as Under 23 Coach.

October 1995. 29 members of the Upper Sixth visited the European

Parliament in Strasbourg as part of the 'Euroscola' Programme. They mixed with students from many different European nationalities and Charlotte Snowdon addressed the whole Assembly in German, explaining what it was like to be a student at Alsager School. This was followed by a debate with many high ranking European civil servants on a number of key European issues. An amazing experience organised by Mr Plant, Mr Halsall and Mrs Keech.

Sixth Form Students visit the European Parliament in Strasbourg 1995.

In the Spring Term of 1997, Rachel Adby, Year 11, was selected for the England Young Elite Golf Squad. She went on to represent England U19s against Wales, Scotland and the Republic of Ireland.

Rachel Adby, England Elite Golf Squad.

Also that term, Bruce Dennison, Year 10, represented Great Britain Gymnastics, in both team and individual events.

It is evident from the above selection of entries that, throughout the eighties and nineties, Alsager dominated inter-school sport in South Cheshire and ranked very highly in Cheshire as a whole. Football, Cross-Country, Netball, Hockey, Athletics, Badminton and Table Tennis were all very strong. During this period, lots of individual students also went on to represent Cheshire in their respective sports.

In July 1997, yet another two Alsager students, Joanne Hughes and David Hughes (no relation), won the Royal Mail Young Letter Writer of the Year Competition. They both won £500 and £700 for the school and had an amazing two days in London. They visited Parliament, had a chartered river cruise, dined at a luxury hotel and were presented with their awards by Jeremey Guscott, the England and British Lions Rugby player and Gladiators presenter. A tremendous, literary achievement and to have both the junior and senior winners from Alsager School!

Joanne Hughes and David Hughes (Standing), Royal Mail Young Letter Writers of the Year with England Rugby Player Jeremy Guscott 1997.

1997 was certainly an excellent year for Alsager students gaining national accolades. Rosie Marshall from Year 8, wrote a speech addressing world leaders at the Rio Earth Summit. Her theme centred on the destruction of the rainforests in the Philippines and was shortlisted for the national final of a competition run by the

Radio Times and the BBC's Newsround programme. Rosie was auditioned at the BBC Television Centre, where she beat three other finalists and won an eight day trip of a lifetime to the Philippines. There, she reported on the rainforest destruction, for a November broadcast on Newsround. How special was that achievement?

During the Autumn of 1997, the work of the school's newly formed Young Engineers Club gained international admiration at the 'Chem Show' in New York. The club was run by Mr Andrew Evans and was formed to encourage boys and girls into engineering and to give them an insight into what the profession entailed. The pupils experienced working to deadlines, liaising with engineers, designing to their specifications and working to industrial standards.

In particular, they worked on a project suggested by the Director of a Liverpool based company, Powder Systems. They produced quarter scale models of equipment, to enable pharmaceutical workers to handle containers of powder more safely. The company was so impressed with these models, that they were featured at the major trade show in New York and also displayed in their Liverpool offices. Enquiries were received from around the USA and Canada and an order was promised from Johnson and Johnson. Quite a remarkable achievement for a group of students aged between 11-16 years. As a thank you, Powder Systems presented the Club with a cheque for £500 to buy new equipment.

In the Summer of 1999, Year 13 student Simon Talbot represented South Cheshire in the Cheshire Athletics Championships at Macclesfield. He won both the 100m and 200m finals, which not only qualified him to represent Cheshire in the inter-counties Mason Trophy Championships at the Alexandra Stadium, Birmingham, but also the English Schools Athletics Championships at Bury St Edmunds. Simon was victorious again in both the 100m and 200m events at Birmingham. Sadly, however, he sustained a serious Achilles injury during the 4x100m relay event, running the final leg, and was not able to finish the race, nor was he able to compete at the English schools Championships. Simon left the Sixth Form to go on to university in South Wales and won a silver medal in 100m at the senior Welsh Athletics Championships.

Excellent student achievements continued into the Millennium.

March 2000, Nathaniel Watts (Year 11) who was the World Champion (U16) in Kumite Karate, won the Junior National Championships in both Kumite and Kata Karate. Nathaniel also won the Congleton Borough Junior Sports Personality of the Year Award for his achievements in karate at World, European and National levels. He was the school's first winner of this award.

2001 got off to a good start with one of our 'A' Level students, Michael Hallsworth, becoming a published author. Michael won a national writing competition from more than a thousand entries, by submitting his impressive short story 'Relativity'. It was based on Einstein's revolutionary theory and chronicled a scientific experiment in space which went horribly wrong. The judges, who included TV Personality Michael Palin, were startled by Michael's talent. The story was published in an anthology called 'The Perfect Journey' which featured all the winning writers and was on the shelves of all the main booksellers next to Harry Potter. Michael went on to study English Literature at Cambridge.

In September 2001 Luke Murphy joined Alsager School from St Mary's Primary in Congleton. Like Lee Bell, Luke was a really talented footballer destined for the professional game. Luke was in my GCSE R.E. group and was keen to do well in his studies. Leaving Alsager in 2006, he went on to captain Crewe Alex before spending 4 seasons at Leeds and then moving on to Bolton Wanderers towards the end of his career.

Also in the Autumn of 2001, Kayleigh Southerton, Year 8, won the BBC 'Passion for Sport' competition. Kayleigh sent in a video to the BBC about her passion for sport. She received a cash prize and went to the BBC Studios to watch a recording of 'A Question of Sport'. She received her prizes from Olympic athlete, Darren Campbell, who visited the school during October. During his visit, I very stupidly challenged him to a sprint up the back drive of school. Needless to say, I came a poor second, but it is something exciting to put in one's CV!

At the same time, Rachel Smith became the U16 National Girls' Archery Champion. Rachel won the championships at East Grinstead on 15th and 16th September shooting the bare bow (no sights).

Samantha Birks, was selected to play golf for Wales against England.

The boys Y8 Rugby Team was undefeated in the Crewe and Nantwich Challenge Tournament. The team scored 62 points and had only 24 points scored against them.

During the Spring 2002, Stephen Heppell was selected to swim for the North West of England, in the National Finals in the U18 butterfly.

Sonja Allen (Year 7) swam in the North Midlands open gala and won the overall competition in her age group. She was then selected for the North Midlands team to swim in regional competitions. In Year 10 Sonja went on to captain the Cheshire Girls Swimming Team to victory in a National Swimming Gala.

Tom Davenport (Year 10) played scrum-half for Staffordshire Schools Rugby. They won 17-5 against North Wales, 12-3 against Mid Wales in the semi-final and 5-0 in the final against South Wales. They won the cup for the first time in Staffordshire's history.

In 2003 Danielle Baker, Alsager's Taekwondo superstar, won a silver medal at the Junior Olympic Games in Detroit. In 2004 she became one of the NSPCC's Champion Children. The tremendous thing was, despite her very rigorous training schedule and lots of travelling, Danielle always managed to keep fully up to date with her school work. In 2006, now in our Sixth Form, Danielle went on to represent Wales at the Commonwealth Taekwondo Championships in Australia, again winning a silver medal. In 2011, Danielle went on to become senior women's National Taekwondo Champion at the 57Kg weight, representing Manchester Aces.

In 2007, another Sixth Form Student, Darcie Worsdale, toured South Africa with the England Under 21 Netball Squad. She then went on to join the Leeds Met Super League squad who appear on Sky Sports.

Also in 2007 at the National English Schools' Swimming Championships, Year 11 Boys finished 3rd in the freestyle medley relay finals and 7th in the medley relay finals. The team comprised Oliver Rabie, Joe Priestman, Scott Hancock and Robert Gaytor. These were marvellous personal achievements and national recognition for the school.

Danielle Baker Commonwealth Taekwondo Silver Medalist and Darcie Worsdale, England U 21 Netball.

March 2008 saw the school's U14 netball team represent the North West of England in the National Schools' Finals at Bournemouth.

In 2009, Ami Pickerill from Year 11 represented England Schools' U19 Netball Team.

In Autumn 2012, the school was blessed with yet another female Taekwondo super star, Chloe Macdonald-Dunn. There must be something in Alsager's water or could it be something to do with the quality of the coaching

The Year 11 Swimming Team.

U14 Netball Squad represented NW England in the National Netball Championships 2008.

Sam Pickford (middle) at the National Swimming Championships (the Olympic Trials) 2012.

at the local clubs? At the International Taekwondo Championships in Belfast, Chloe won a gold medal in the Under 17 category, although only 14 years old at the time. A delighted Chloe said:

"Receiving the gold medal was extremely special, as it was presented by Master Shin, the Grand Master of Taekwondo, who has been practising the sport for over 40 years".

Again in Autumn 2012, Sixth Former Sam Pickford competed in the National Swimming Championships (effectively the Olympic Trials) in Sheffield, rubbing shoulders with the likes of Rebecca Adlington and world record holder, Liam Tancock. He had achieved 3 national qualifying times, one of which was good enough to take him to these finals. Sam was captain of the then, Alsager Bridgestones Swimming Club and was delighted to have made the finals, which was a fantastic experience for him.

Mr Andrew Wishart, who was Head of Year 12 at the time said that:

"Sam was an outstanding student, who managed to combine a gruelling training schedule with an excellent performance and attitude in all his 'A' Level studies".

Sam seems to be one of those young people who is living proof of the 'age-old adage' that those who are often the most successful and fulfilled in life, are those who 'work hard and play hard'.

Extraordinary Talent in Performing Arts

Throughout its history as a secondary modern and comprehensive school, Alsager has had a strong tradition in Music and Drama.

Successive Heads of Music always encouraged and developed instrumental and choral skills and gave students a range of extra-curricular opportunities in which to perform, either in the Hollinshead Hall, local Churches or at more prestigious venues further afield. The school also benefited from the fact that many of its students, with an interest in leaning to play a musical instrument, were able to access private tuition from within the community. As a result the school's orchestras, brass bands and ensembles were always a joy to listen to at concerts. Equally, choirs were splendidly rehearsed and sang in auditoriums like the Liverpool Philharmonic and Bridgewater Halls.

When I first arrived at Alsager, Alan Baker was the Head of Music. Other members of staff to hold the position down the years included - Keith Mosedale, Heather Bridger, John Turner, Michelle Bridgett, Sandra Wallace, Paul Morley and Vince Galley.

Many outstanding musicians graced our concerts, some of whom went on to study music and follow careers in the profession. Margaret Ozanne studied Music at Oxford and went on to become a concert pianist, playing at many of the UK's most prestigious venues. Peter Godfrey, an outstanding flautist at school, reached the final stages of the BBC's Young Musician of the Year in 1982. Robert Hindmarsh and Andrew Robinson were superb violinists and played from an early age in the Cheshire Youth orchestra. I well remember Robert and Andrew playing various violin concertos at school concerts and being in awe of their skill and the sound they produced. The violin had always been my favourite instrument, as

I had played it in the East Glamorgan Youth Orchestra many, many years before. Not quite like Robert and Andrew, I hasten to add!

Talented flautist

Peter Godfrey, Semi-finalist BBC Young Musician of the Year 1982.

Claire Hampton was a wonderful singer in school. At 14 years of age, she joined the National Youth Choir of Great Britain and later studied at the Royal Northern College of Music. She worked as a freelance singer until joining Welsh National Opera in 2002. Claire's personal highlights at the WNO so far have been performing the role of Papagena in The Magic Flute, Jana in Jenůfa and walking the red carpet as Marilyn Monroe. Two other great musical talents at school were Dr Ben Hamilton and Daniel Keen.

Ben Hamilton is currently Musical Director of a number of amateur choirs, including the Cheshire Fire Service Choir, the Urbe Choir and the Warwickshire Choristers. He is also a guest conductor at operas around the UK.

Daniel Keen has his own successful music company, Sandbach Music. He is one of the organisers of the Alsager Music Festival, Musical Director of the Alsager Community Choir and Principal Cornet with Audley Brass. His personal highlights include: performing at the London 2012 Olympic Opening Ceremony, conducting numerous brass bands and orchestras around the UK, including Fodens Brass and the Amadeus and West Yorkshire Symphony Orchestras. He has also organised many concerts and performed several with Julian Lloyd-Webber. Other star performers at school were Ian Harding, Oliver Duerden, Josh and Noah Eve, Hilary Large and Stephanie Jones.

School Musicians play at Alsager Community Theatre's Annual Open Production at Little Moreton Hall circa 1985.

May 9th 1981, 8 Alsager pupils performed with Cheshire Youth Orchestra, at the Lyceum Crewe.

8th and 9th 1986. The Swing Band and Brass Bands were invited to play at the Stoke on Trent Garden Festival on both afternoons.

On March 29th 1990, the school Brass Quintet of Mark Cadman,

Richard Parkinson (trumpets), Patrick Buckley (tuba), James Seddon (horn) and Richard Harding (trombone) reached the final of National Brass Festival of Brass Ensembles, at the Queen Elizabeth Hall, London. They were one of ten finalists from all over the country but remarkably they were the only comprehensive school. Competitors were of the ilk of the Wells Cathedral School, the Guildhall School of Music and the Birmingham Schools Ensemble. We came third.

Alsager School Brass Quintet 1990 Finalists at Queen Elizabeth Hall, London.

November 25th 1990, The Senior Choir performed Verdi's Requiem at the Liverpool Philharmonic Hall.

On 15th November 1991 the Alsager School Orchestra and the Cheshire Constabulary Band presented its 'Kops n' Kids' concert. Certainly a night to remember in a packed Hollinshead Hall.

From 1992 onwards Josephine Large, Davinia Caddy and Julia Seddon were a trio of wonderful musicians who featured prominently in school concerts throughout that period. Josephine went on to study at the Royal College of Music and is now co-principal percussionist in the Liverpool Philharmonic Orchestra. Davinia Caddy, a flautist, went on to study Music at Chethams

Davinia Caddy and Josephine Large.

School of Music, Manchester, and then Selwyn College, Cambridge, before taking up a lecturing post at the University of Auckland. Throughout 1993-94, Davinia, then in Year 10, was a member of the National Children's Youth Orchestra, playing flute and piccolo. To become a member, she had to audition with hundreds of other young musicians from across the UK, to have the opportunity to play in a full symphony orchestra. Davinia played in many of the nation's great concert halls, including the Royal Albert Hall, the Royal Festival Hall and the Queen Elizabeth Hall. At the Schools' Prom, the orchestra concluded the evening's performance,

CHESHIRE CONSTABULARY JUVENILE DEPARTMENT
present

IN ALSAGER

WITH THE CHESHIRE CONSTABULARY BAND
AT ALSAGER COMPREHENSIVE SCHOOL
Friday, 15th November, 1991 at 7.30 p.m.

Front page of the Kops n' Kids programme.

with Edward Elgar's Pomp and Circumstance, March No 1 - Land of Hope and Glory. How amazing to be part of such a finale. Both Davinia and Josephine Large won places in the National Youth Orchestra in 1995, when they were in Year 11.

More recently Jakob Scoffield, a bass guitar player, went to study music at the Royal Northern College of Music. Brothers Josh and Luke Prince, a drummer and saxophonist respectively went to the Leeds College of Music, while Tim Hargreaves, a guitarist, who figured prominently in all our concerts and shows, went to Warwick to study Maths. Esme Turner was another wonderful flautist who was a joy to listen to at all our concerts.

Equally spectacular over the years were the school's drama productions which included:

- The Snow Queen
- Under Milk Wood
- A Midsummer Night's Dream
- Blood Brothers
- Oaklahoma
- Wizard of Oz
- Return to the Forbidden Planet
- Our Day Out
- Bugsy Malone
- Numerous Alan Ayckbourn plays

- Cider with Rosie
- Oliver
- Hairspray
- Seussical
- We Will Rock You
- Grease
- Hot Mikado
- The Wiz
- Teechers
- Annie

The Snow Queen. Alsager Secondary School's first full production 1964. Produced by M Shemilt.

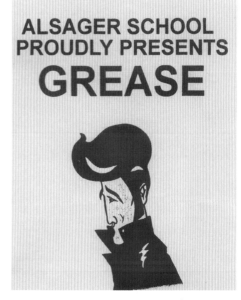

Programme for Grease.

The cast of Oliver 2018.

The cast of Return to the Forbidden Planet.

Heads of Drama over the years were Keith Plant, Anne Hardcastle, Diane Garrett (Thomas), Julie Betts-Nicholson, Phil Redford, Esther Gardener and Steph Wise.

The productions took a great deal of team work with Music, Drama, Art, and Technology all working together, not to mention other individual members of staff who supported behind the scenes. One such person was the Head of the English Faculty, Graham Shaw, who always worked tirelessly on sound and lighting. Over many years he had two student assistants who went on to accomplish great things in the field of Stage Management. The first student was Warren Barlow who set up two companies providing stage management equipment for shows and events, one in the UK and one in Dubai. The second student was Duncan Hook, who spent a gap year as a Drama Technician at school before going on to study Stage Management at The Royal Academy of Dramatic Arts (RADA). He became a stage manager in the West End, involved with box office successes such as Jersey Boys, Wizard of OZ, Love Never Dies, Rock of Ages and Stephen Ward.

The leads in some of these wonderful school productions included Rachel Hubble, Penelope Beech, Liam Davey, Nick Evans, Gaynor Edwards and Fiona O'Mahoney in the first Grease; Sally Brooks in the Wizard of OZ and Oaklahoma; Will Henshall in Bugsy and We will Rock You; Andy O'Rourke, Jack Stancliffe, Jade Kelsall, Maddie Gregory, Will Henshall and Hope Bristow in Return to the Forbidden Planet; Lois Smith in Grease; Molly Brown in the Wiz, Hot Mikado and Hairspray; Alex Jacob in The Wiz and Hairspray; Mollie Wedgewood in Seussical, Hot Mikado, Grease, Annie; Caitlin Hamilton Seussical, Grease, Annie. Other leads included: Poppy Devenport, Phoebe Cooke, Jacob Unwin, Esmaie Doig, Jenny Rowles, Andreya Georgiou, Olivia Warburton, Megan Lander, Jakob Harper and Charlotte Myatt.

Cider with Rosie stars, Jonathon Williams, Elizabeth Doel and Jack Stancliffe.

The Cast of the Hot Mikado.

They provided so much enjoyment over many years. It was worth becoming a Governor of Alsager School, simply to have a front row seat, to see such talented young people in shows and concerts! When individual students such as these left the school, there was always a note of regret and a feeling that such talent could never be replaced. But the reality about Alsager was and is that talent of the highest order seems to be a recurring feature of school life. No sooner have our young people moved on, to pursue their careers beyond school, then others 'step up to the mark', with an equal ability to entertain and enthral, for another five or seven years.

For a number of years in the early eighties there was even a staff drama group which put on annual productions, often directed by Keith Plant. In the nineties and into the millennium the staff pantomimes were always a 'hoot' in the lead up to Christmas, with Tony Clare and Chris Davies 'leading lights'. There were many funny, raucous moments but the one that stands out for me involves long serving French teacher, Trevor Sparrow. He leapt onto the stage, fully regaled in dinner jacket, arms straight and pointing at the audience, gun in hand. He delivered his lines impressively. *"I'm Bond, James Bond"*. From one of the front rows, a squeaky little voice barked back. *"No you're not you're Trevor"*. The Hall fell apart with laughter. Fun times.

Productions, however were not confined to the era of comprehensive education. Quite lavish performances were staged during the period when the school was a secondary modern. Archive photographs like the one below bear witness to the impressive nature of the staging and the quality of the costumes circa 1962.

School Production in the Old School Hall c.1962.

Poetry Corner was the result of an idea by former English teacher, Steve Smith, who wrote the following about one of his students.

"We pride ourselves in celebrating cultural differences and diverse backgrounds in language studies. Sometimes this throws up an exciting and innovative piece of creative writing, like this poem from an English born thirteen year old boy, with Welsh family roots. His name is Bryn Phillips".

Bryn Phillips receiving his English Award for Excellence for his poem, from teacher Steve Smith.

A Battle Inside
Wales versus England

Bryn is a Welsh name,
In an English county,
My split self,
Whose side am I on?
Mum likes the rivalry of football,
Dad likes the adrenalin of rugby,
My split self,
Whose side am I on?
Most people say goodnight,
I say nos da,
My split self,
Whose side am I on?
My first words were "un dau tri"
Whereas others say "mummy" or "daddy",
My split self,
Whose side am I on?
But in the end there is no doubt,
I know where my heart lies,
WALES!!

Like Steve Smith, I thought it was an innovative piece of writing which I had to include in my book. Moving from South Wales to Alsager 42 years ago, I can empathise with Bryn completely. Whose side am I on? I only came for 5 years and here I am, still here! Whose side am I on now? Like Bryn's Dad, I love rugby, particularly Welsh rugby. I played for Pontypridd as a young man, before moving to Cheshire. Mark Cueto was from my school, my student and my friend. With his parents, I watched him play for Sale Sharks against Pontypridd in the Parker Pen Cup Final and of course for England against Wales, I was his most ardent supporter. Whose side am I on Bryn? I sat in Congleton Rugby Club and watched England lose to South Africa in the 2019 World Cup Final, 100% behind England. But what if Wales had beaten South Africa, as they could well have done, in the last few minutes of their semi-final? Whose side would

I have been on Bryn? "But in the end without a doubt", like Bryn, "I know where my heart lies. WALES!!"

Individual students have always excelled and gone on to achieve great things in many different walks of life beyond school - in business, in specific trades, in the arts, in academia, in sport, in medicine, journalism, to mention but a few categories. As a school we have been proud of them all. At this point, I would like to mention just four, simply because, one I know as a friend, one I taught for O and A Level Geography, while the careers of the remaining two, I have followed through television and the press.

The first is the England and British and Irish Lions Rugby player, Mark Cueto. He played 55 times for England on the wing and in that position he is the third highest try scorer of all time, scoring 20 tries. He also scored one of the most famous and debated tries of all time, in the World Cup Final of 2007. Sadly it was disallowed and England lost to South Africa, 15-6. However, the debate continues, as the TV official, because of a language barrier, was denied access to frame by frame pictures, which could have proved more conclusively whether Mark had actually put his foot in touch, before scoring the try. Until very

Mark Cueto celebrating after receiving his MBE.

recently when his record was beaten, Mark was the top try scorer in the English Rugby Premier League. With his Mum and Dad, I had the privilege of watching Mark play for Sale Sharks and England on many occasions. On 15th March 2016, Mark's achievements were recognised when he was invested with the MBE by Prince William at Buckingham Palace, for services to Rugby Union.

The Second is Professor David Bailey, who is an academic economist at the Birmingham Business School. He has a very high media profile. Look out for him on the BBC News, as he is often the BBC's 'go to' person on a range of economic issues. His numerous roles make him one of the most influential people in the Midlands Region. He is a great defender of British Manufacturing Industry and has led a number of campaigns to defend it, pushing for greater protection from the Government.

David was one of the most outstanding students I ever taught, in all my years at Alsager and one of the most unassuming young people.

The Third former student is Jane Standley, who studied Languages and English before going on to university. Our time at Alsager only crossed for a short while, as Jane left a few years after I arrived, but I became aware of her through my good friend Mair Needham, who was her Head of Year and very close to Jane. As a result, I followed Jane's career at the BBC.

In 1994-2001 Jane was the BBC's Africa correspondent. She will be most remembered for her coverage of the genocide in Rwanda-Burundi. I will never forget a programme she covered for BBC 2 on the worst of the atrocities, it was heart breaking and a fantastic piece of journalism. She received all sorts of awards, including the MBE for 'services to journalism'. Jane went on to become the BBC's correspondent in New York and covered 9/11 for which she received an Emmy Award. Jane has also been an advocate of equal pay for women, which was the reason she eventually quit the BBC after 18 years. Truly, one of our country's greatest journalists.

Finally, there is Kate Dennison, sister of Simon and Bruce mentioned earlier in this chapter. Another great Alsager sporting family. Kate was the first British Junior Pole Vaulter to jump 4.0 metres. She then went on to represent England at the 2006 Commonwealth Games, where she came 7th. She represented Great Britain at the Beijing Olympics in 2008, came 4th in the European Championships in 2009 and won a Bronze Medal in the 2010 Commonwealth Games in

New Delhi. She has been the British Pole Vault Record Holder both indoors and outdoors and broke the outdoor record 9 times in 8 months. A really outstanding athlete.

Chapter 6: A New Head: A New Way of Thinking

Mr Black began his Headship at the start of the Autumn Term 1993.

On 4th October after his first month in post, he wrote:

"It has been a full and enjoyable month. Everybody has been friendly and supportive. My feet have hardly touched the ground!.....Exam results were excellent... The A Level Results have placed us in the top 10 Comprehensives nationally again".

One of the earliest changes implemented by Mr Black, which took effect from September 1994, was the move to a 'diagnostic' first year. Previously, the school had been arranged in ability 'bands'. For instance, if a particular year was 10 form- entry, there may have been 7 'band one' classes and 3 'band two' classes. Pupils would have been taught in those bands for all subjects. Within the upper band, different subjects would have had different setting arrangements. Some subjects would have had tight setting - 1,2,3, for example, others much broader arrangements. Pupils would also have remained in their bands for form periods. Whether a child went into Band one or two was dependent on their performance in the Cheshire Tests, in the final year at primary school.

A diagnostic first year, gave all pupils the chance to settle more effectively, in 'mixed ability' form groups and show their abilities and skills in the different subjects. After a period of time in the first year, there was some broad setting in maths and modern foreign languages. Beyond the first year, setting was introduced according to the demands of individual subjects, as pupils moved through the school. There was movement between sets and pupils could be in higher sets for those subjects in which they showed the greatest promise.

Believe me, this represented, not only a significant change in school structure but also a philosophical change of some magnitude. A courageous move on Mr Black's part, as there were a good many staff to win over, not to mention some governors.

The school had always done a great deal of work to raise money for local, national and international charities. Year groups and form groups would take on fund raising activities and relatively small amounts of money would be raised from many different quarters of the school. In September 1994, it was decided that charitable fund raising, of this kind, should be more co-ordinated and it was agreed that Year 8 and the Sixth Form would take on this role each year.

Shirley Cross with some of her Year 8 students who raised £9000 for the North Staffordshire Hospital 1994.

The first Year 8 to take on this task was led by Senior Tutor, Shirley Cross and she and her team of tutors embarked on this 'crusade' with gusto, determination and a great deal of imagination. Shirley believed that this was a vital aspect of school life:

"Young people, working in the broader community, doing worthwhile things for others, gaining experiences that they will remember for the rest of their lives".

Most weekends, Shirley was out and about in the village, with groups of her Year, persuading people to part with their money. There was a splendid Christmas Fair, with a huge cake stall and even an enormous Chinese Dragon dancing around the school yard, at one stage. The outcome of all of these activities was around £9,000 raised in a nine month period. The students decided that the funds raised should go to the Paediatrics Department at the North Staffs Hospital, to purchase a domiciliary ventilator, an ECG machine for the new Paediatric Intensive Care Ambulance and a specialist treatment couch for Cystic Fibrosis patients. At the end of the Summer Term, hospital staff were presented with a large cheque at a ceremony at school.

Other Heads of Year, followed in Shirley's footsteps. Mike Elkin came up with the novel idea of giving each member of his year group £1 and the enterprising challenge to 'make it grow'. This became a blueprint for future fund-raising plans.

Parent 'Attitude towards school' surveys are fairly common place in today's schools, but back in the Nineties, surveys of this nature were fairly rare. In the Summer Term of 1995, Alsager School Governors commissioned Keele University to undertake a survey of the attitudes of Alsager parents to the school. Approximately 25% of parents were sent a questionnaire and some of the results appear below.

- 98% would recommend the school to friends
- 99% thought the educational standards achieved were good or very good
- 91% thought buildings were in good condition
- 96% approved of the quality of the information they received about their child's progress
- Only 51% knew enough about the National Curriculum
- 96% of parents said they were made to feel welcome by the school
- 95% said teachers were approachable
- 55% expressed concern about tolerance of bad behaviour
- 17% felt discipline could be stricter
- 90% said their child was happy at school
- 95% were satisfied with the progress their child was making

Following on from the survey, the school newspaper, 'Headlines', appeared once per month, specific parent information evenings were held on aspects of the National Curriculum and articles on the educational changes of the day also appeared regularly in the newspaper.

When I arrived at Alsager School in 1978, there was already a large Adult Education Centre based at the school, with a wide variety of classes on offer two evenings per week. Although it was based at the school, it was organised by Cheshire County Council, funded by Central Government and managed by one of our long serving Technology teachers, Mr Trevor Worsley. In 1991, by the time Mr Worsley retired, the organisation of Adult Education had been taken over by South Cheshire College and a joint appointment was agreed of a teacher/adult education manager, to take over the day to day management of the classes. The person appointed was Margaret Lawson and in our Autumn 1995 school newsletter, she advertised the new and existing classes on offer for January 1996. These included - basic keyboard skills, computing in retirement, calligraphy, yoga, shiatsu and tai chi, cookery, Indian cookery, sugar craft, GCSE Psychology, painting and drawing, Japanese, French, German, Italian, Spanish and, I'm glad to say, Welsh. Quite an impressive array.

The problem was, by this time, South Cheshire College was under pressure from the Government, through its funding mechanism, to offer as many 'schedule 2' classes as possible. These were classes which led directly to recognised qualifications, rather than recreational classes, offered for pleasure. As a result, numbers registering for adult classes began to fall, to the point where South Cheshire invited Alsager U3A to take over some of the 'non schedule 2' classes for pleasure. They also offered U3A free use of the classrooms at the school. Ultimately, David Collins, the Principal at South Cheshire, 'pulled the plug' on Adult Education at Alsager School and it never re-appeared. U3A, on the other hand, flourished and has continued to do so to the present day.

School Funding in Cheshire East has been a current issue for Mr Middlebrook and the Governors, for a good many years. Many of you will know from articles in the local press and information Mr Middlebrook has sent home, that Cheshire East is one of the most poorly funded Local Authorities in England, under the existing National Funding Formula.

You may be interested to know, that this funding issue has been a problem for Alsager School and other Cheshire schools for a very long time. In October 1996, David Black wrote:

"Schools in Cheshire are faced with the prospect of a cut of £6.1 million in their budgets next year, unless there is quick and effective action now. For many years, Cheshire has been treated unfairly, in the way that national budgets have been divided amongst Local Authorities. Money has been directed away from Cheshire in favour of London and the South East. The injustice in the current process has been recognised now by an independent review body set up by the Government. This body estimated that to help fund local services, Cheshire deserves an additional £18 million- money that is retained in the South. For education, this translates into an additional £4.925 million for secondary schools and £4.5m for primary schools.

If we are unable to persuade Government to accept the recommendations of the review we will need to impose cuts of 3.9%, which would mean a loss of £118,000 for this school next year. This in turn would result in a loss of teachers, larger classes, fewer courses available and so on".

Desperate words indeed from David Black and if you cast your mind back to 1981, Jim Andrews was saying more or less the same thing. Fast forward now to 2019-20 and Richard Middlebrook, is still faced with the reality of a student in a secondary school in semi-rural Berkshire or Oxfordshire, commanding far greater funding than a student at Alsager School, in semi-rural East Cheshire. Little has changed!

From the mid-Nineties, Mr Black and the Leadership Team began thinking about more innovative roles for key members of the support staff within the school. Traditionally, these roles had been undertaken by senior teaching staff, often by Deputy Heads. For instance, cover for absent staff, personnel responsibilities, ICT and data management, management of the finances and so on. If these roles could be carried out by non-teachers, then our most experienced teachers, would be more available to focus on the core business of making learning and teaching more effective.

Again there was some scepticism over this idea at first, but the support staff appointed to these roles were first rate and fitted in seamlessly. A key person in this re-modelling process was Annette Owen who joined the school in 1994 as Mr Black's PA. She went on to become the school's first Personnel and Projects Manager. In the 25 years Mrs Owen was at the school, the number of support staff increased from fewer than twenty five to around sixty five. Shortly after Mrs Owen's appointment, Carys Dougill became Finance Manager and other posts spiralled in all sorts of different areas of school support - IT, Data, Learning Resource Centre Manager, Cover Manager and Cover Supervisors, School Counsellor, Site Manager, Exam Administrator, Vocational Co-ordinator, Attendance and Inclusion Manager and Reprographics Manager. The Personnel and Finance Managers were on the Senior Leadership Team and many support staff were involved with student life as well as their administrative roles.

Alsager really was in the vanguard of change in this area and led the way throughout Cheshire, with many schools trying to incorporate its model for school administration. Again, Mr Black must be credited for his innovative thinking and inclusive management style.

1996 saw Alsager School and indeed the town of Alsager, achieve another milestone. Twenty five years of Comprehensive Education. To celebrate this landmark, the PTA held a Silver Jubilee Dance in the Hollinshead Hall, on Saturday 22nd June. It was very well attended and it was hard to decide whether this was due to the 'nostalgia' of

Mike Elkin and Doug Barnet. Their 25 years of service corresponded with the Anniversary of 25 Years of Comprehensive Education at Alsager School in 1996.

the Silver Jubilee or the pulling power of XL5, Andy Pennance's sixties rock band. In any event, the evening was a great success.

In September 1997, for the very first time, girls were allowed to wear 'black tailored' school trousers. These had to be standard in design and were not to be leggings, cords, flairs, denims, chinos or any form of fashion trousers. This issue had been debated by the Student Council the previous year and agreed.

In May 1998 the PE faculty, under the leadership of Sonia Cross, was awarded the prestigious Sportsmark Award for the quality of its curriculum. The award was given by the English Sports Council to schools which offered a wide range of competitive and non-competitive sports. They had to have good facilities, good participation rates and run competitive games within the school, as well as competing with other schools. This was a great achievement for the PE staff and the many other staff who contributed to extra-curricular sport.

Throughout the Summer of 1998, the school began a major investment programme in Information Technology. This was supported, very generously, by over £70,000 of donations from local companies, Friends of the School and an £11,000 contribution from the PTA. Significant extensions were made to our computer facilities and our old library was transformed into a 'state of the art' Learning Resource Centre, The LRC, as it is still affectionately known, was officially opened by Anne Winterton MP. on 23rd October 1998. Parents were then invited to an LRC Open Evening, on Tuesday 3rd November, to view the new facilities. The facility was opened on Tuesday evenings, for the community to use the computer/internet resources.

Another area where Alsager was 'well ahead of the game' in terms of its thinking, was in the development of its Pastoral Systems. Traditionally, the school had been organised on a Year Group basis. Each year was led by a Head of Year (called a Senior Tutor) and a team of tutors, who moved with the students through the school from Year 7 to Year 11. The Sixth Form always had its own Director of Sixth Form and team of tutors. These Senior Tutors were strong but caring teachers who had an extremely positive influence over their year groups. The one downside with the system was the time they had to do the job. Although they were given additional non-teaching time, it was never enough to fulfil the role, as they would want.

Having been a topic of discussion for quite some time, in September 2005, Alsager School created a new pastoral structure based on 4 'vertical' Colleges, rather than 'horizontal' years. The Colleges were called Dod, Lovell, Moreton and Royce. In each College there would be 2 or 3 forms from each year group, depending on how many forms there were in a particular year. What was special about this re structuring, was that the school would work towards a situation where eventually, all the new College Managers were to be non-teachers, who could devote all of their time to the needs of the students. Again, that idea of using 'adults other than teachers' in a key role within the school.

Following on from the College re-structuring, Autumn Term 2006 saw the introduction of College Councils, with students from all years invited to apply for the roles. At the council meetings, they would be expected to represent the views of their forms and work collaboratively with their peers and Heads of Colleges. Students now had the chance to shape their experience of being members of Alsager School, through a forum that really counted. A total of 73 applications were received prior to the secret ballot within Colleges. All representatives received formal training on how to be an effective council member, at the conference centre at Twyfords.

In January 2000 Mr Black was seconded to Stanney High School, Ellesmere Port, for two terms. Mr Philip Clarke became Acting Head, supported by Mr Austen and myself in running the school.

On February 4th 2000, the PTA held its Millennium Auction in the Hollinshead Hall. There were over 80 pledges of gifts, activities and services to suit the tastes of everyone from the young to the not so young, the adventurous to the less adventurous. More specifically you could have bid for a bungee jump, a microlight flight, a meal cooked by a professional chef, paintings by local artists including, Caroline Bailey, a chauffeured trip to Cardiff's Millennium Stadium, to see Wales play an international rugby match and a few hours ironing and baby-sitting. On the evening, I bid for a half tonne of manure to replenish my borders. Quite a frightening sight when it is dumped on your front drive and you have to move it into the back garden!

The evening was a great success, with auctioneer Mr Richard Peake, in charge of proceedings. On this occasion, parents did us proud, with £4500 being raised on the night, for the refurbishment of the School Medical Suite.

For many years the school, unlike most schools, had been in the fortunate position of being able to employ its own, full time, school nurse who was worth her weight in gold, not only to the students but also to staff. During this period our nurses were Pat Edwards and Tricia Heaton. Pat Edwards was in post for a very long time, for not only was she employed permanently by the school from Easter 1991 to December 1995, she had been employed by the Health Authority and based at the school since 1979. Pat was a real 'angel of mercy' to me personally. On occasions, I would come into school on a Monday with rugby injuries which had involved stitches. Not only would Pat regularly clean my wounds but also, very gently, she would take out my stitches when required, so saving a dreaded return visit to hospital.

I feel indebted to the Edwards family to this day, not just for Pat's care over many years, but also to her husband Jim. He was Deputy Head for a number of years during the 1970s and, with Jim Andrews and Ian Macpherson, appointed me as Head of Geography in 1978.

PTA events were not always as well attended as the Millennium Auction. For many years, throughout the Nineties and into the Millennium, the PTA struggled to get parent participation, which was quite frustrating for those active members of the committee. Two notable exceptions, were the Annual Craft Fair and the Plant Sale which always did well in terms of attendance and financial returns. The driving force behind both the Millennium Auction and the many Craft fairs was our Personnel Manager, Mrs Annette Owen, probably the most organised person on the planet. The school owes a great debt to her and all those parents and staff, who supported and propped up the PTA over many years, through to about 2005, when it finally folded.

Recently, found archive material pinpointed the origins of the PTA to the 1st October 1959 and the initiative of Headteacher, Mr Parker. An article in 'The Times' noted that:

"The Headmaster of Alsager Secondary Modern School, Mr F.G. Parker, is anxious to form a liaison between the child's home and the school and is at present exploring the possibilities of forming a Parent-Teacher Association, to help children receive continual guidance".

So we have Mr Hawkes to thank for the Swan logo, which did stand the test of time to this day and Mr Parker to thank for the many years of 'sterling' work from the PTA, which sadly did not!

While on the subject of the PTA, there was one other event worthy of note, as it was the only PTA event in history, which was a complete sell out. It was a joint concert performed by the Audley Male Voice Choir and the Alsager School Orchestra, on 2nd February 2002, in the Hollinshead Hall. It was a superb concert, led by Philip Broadbent, Musical Director of The Audley and Paul Morley and Andrew Welsh of the school's Music Department. Compares for the evening were 'yours truly' and the greatly missed, Jill Bristow, Alsager's answer to 'Phil and Holly'. So successful was the concert and so delighted was The Audley with their reception, that the event was repeated in February 2003. £1200 was raised for PTA funds.

PTA Cheque Presentation to Christie Hospital, 29th February 1988, with Liz Burkinshaw Chair, Anne Reynolds, Secretary, Chris Morris and Mike Elkin.

Throughout the late Eighties, Nineties and into the Millennium, a feature of life at Alsager School, and other schools in Cheshire, was the Work Experience Programme for students in Year 10. This was part of the wider Careers Education Programme, run for many years by Mrs Bette Pointon, with the work experience package organised by Ms Pat Sutton and then Mrs Cath Hayter. The work experience was supported by the Cheshire Careers Service for many years but in 2002 a new, independent, organisation 'Connexions' was created. This brought together a whole range of support services for students, in the form of Vocational and Personal Guidance.

Organising work placements for 250 or so students was a mammoth undertaking which took months of preparation and many last minute re-adjustments. I did not envy Ms Sutton's and Mrs Hayter's task. In the school newsletter 'Headlines' for March/April 2000, Ms Sutton wrote the following comments:

"Once again our Year 10 pupils, full of trepidation, entered the world of work for two weeks. The placements were many and varied - from being a vet's assistant to working at the Alexandra Soccer Centre".

"When a teacher rang an employer to check on one pupil's progress, the reply was complimentary but with a reservation - the pupil had failed to arrive on time occasionally. Further inquiries revealed that the boy was expected to arrive for a 7.00 am. start at a farm some miles from his home. Happily, this placement went very well, but it does illustrate how pupils have to adapt and show resilience. Farmers start early and farming is physically hard work!"

"Others were working in the evenings, assisting with performances at the Crewe Lyceum, with others having to cope with being called 'Sir' and 'Miss' at local primary schools. One girl did her experience in South Africa. Needless to say, she received no personal visit from her teachers!"

"Our thanks go to all those industrialists who participated in our Team Building Day, in the Hollinshead Hall, leading up to work experience. Again, they commented how smart our pupils looked in their business dress and how engaged they were in the day's activities. They were a credit to the school".

On April 26th 2000 the school gained the 'Investors in People' Award. This was a prestigious award which reflected the commitment the school made, and continues to make, to the well-being of its staff. Led by Deputy Head, Hedley Austen, the school had been working for two years to demonstrate effective communication, training and staff development, and a leadership style, which valued all staff for the contribution they made to the life and work of the school.

June 6th 2000 Mr Purcell and Mr Austen and two Sixth Form Students, Sarah Groom and Tim Peake, visited the Barbican in London to receive another prestigious award - the National Schools' Curriculum Award.

Also in June 2000, Alsager School became one of 33 secondary schools nationally, to be awarded 'Training School' Status by the Government. This was in recognition of the quality of the work it was undertaking, in conjunction with Keele University, in training graduates about to enter the teaching profession.

The award enabled the school to access additional funds from the DfEE to develop an 'innovative classroom' which had state of the art learning resources. Most exciting of which were the interactive white boards and networked PCs. Although primarily targeted at teacher training, the facilities were used by pupils within the school, so that the impact of new technologies could be evaluated. Keith Plant became the new Director of the Training School and the 'innovative classroom' was housed in the 'Yellow Room' PE3, adjacent to the school entrance.

During the Summer break of 2000, the Astro pitch surface was replaced.

Mr Black returned from Stanney High School in September 2000 and stated in the log:

"The school has continued to thrive in my absence".

It had thrived to the point where it was in a similar position to that of today, in that we were heavily over-subscribed and faced the unpleasant prospect of having to turn pupils and families away.

Governors had agreed to admit 252 pupils, although our planned admissions number was actually 225. The situation in the Sixth Form was one of continued growth and we had 280 students following 'A' Level courses, with 158 of these in Year 12. The school was 'bulging at the seams', with the prospect of over 1600 on roll the following year.

To cope with this increasing roll, the Governors agreed to appoint 4 new teachers and the Local Authority had agreed the previous year, to part fund an additional 5 classrooms, in a new building. This was part of the deal, linked to Mr Black's secondment to Stanney High School. The school's budget also provided some of the funding. Additional PE changing facilities were also provided in a separate building, again jointly funded by Cheshire, Congleton Borough and the School. The block of classrooms provided new accommodation for the Maths Department originally, and was named after retired, long-serving, Senior Tutor Mike Elkin, who taught at the school from 1961 to 1997. The new changing rooms were named after Medwyn Jones who for many years was Head of PE at the school.

Sonia Cross, Head of PE and Philip Clarke, Deputy Head outside the new Medwyn Jones changing facilities.

During the Autumn Term of 2000, there had been much discussion amongst Messrs Black, Clarke, Austen and myself about the possibility of extending the Senior Leadership Team. It was felt that this would give that extra capacity to drive forward further developments and improvements. As a result, in December 2000, Jill Bristow, Keith Plant and Mel Smith were appointed to this team as Assistant Heads. For the first time, the Assistant Head role appeared in the staffing structure, which offered aspiring staff additional, internal promotion prospects.

September 2002 saw the school attempt to modernise the school uniform, introducing pale blue polo shirts and abandoning white shirts and ties. Mr Black in his Head's report to parents 2003-4 wrote:

"It seems hard to remember now, but 12 months ago was a time when a great many people were concerned about the introduction of our school polo shirts. Now that a year has passed and we can see all of key stage 3 and key stage 4 wearing the new shirts, I hope you feel as I do, that the students don't look too bad at all. I would not argue with anyone that a shirt and tie worn properly is smarter than an open neck polo shirt. The problem was that we were never able to get 100% of students wearing their ties and shirts properly. As one Sixth Former, who attended the Governors meetings, put it 'Polo shirts are less smart than a shirt and tie but overall the school looks better because the appearance of pupils is more uniform'."

Personally, I was never a great fan of the new uniform and felt we should have tried harder to get students to smarten the way they wore their blazers, shirts and ties. Today's students, having reverted to the more traditional uniform, with the maroon blazer and clip tie, look much smarter, in my opinion.

2003 heralded a change to the pattern of the school day. This was a major event for many staff and pupils and it would be it foolish to deny that there was a certain amount of discontent, particularly over cutting the lunch break from 60 to 45 minutes. At the end of the consultation process, Governors took the view that the proposed change was in the wider interest of the school and students and the change was implemented. Although a review of the change was agreed for the Spring Term 2004.

A cost benefit analysis was carried out shortly after the changes were implemented and the following feedback was reported.

Benefits

- Higher quality assemblies.
- Split lunch breaks made much better use of the school's limited canteen facilities.
- Queues in the canteens were shorter.
- Litter was much reduced.
- The campus was much calmer at lunchtime and there were fewer disciplinary problems.
- Students were able to get to village and back in 40 minutes because queues in village were shorter.
- Owners of food outlets liked the new system because students did not all arrive at once.
- Members of the public said that it was better as pupils did not all swarm out of school at once - less congestion on pavements and safer for students.
- Music practices worked well.
- The Year 11 social space was used well and appropriately.

Costs

- Staff found morning registration too short - only 5 minutes
- Senior Tutors found it difficult to see pupils/contact parents in the morning because of insufficient time.
- Communication between staff was not so easy because of the shorter lunch break.

During 2002, the school began to develop a link with Oshilemba School, a school in Northern Namibia. At the end of October 2003, Mr Black wrote:

"I was very privileged to be able to visit our partner school in Northern Namibia. Three weeks were spent travelling, training and

teaching in a country, the like of which I have never visited before. The lessons for me were profound and there can be nothing better to make you appreciate what you have, than to teach in an African school. Work continues to develop and extend the partnership. Letters have been exchanged between students, and Ms Sutton and Mrs Woods will be exchanging with two Namibian teachers in the summer. This teacher exchange is an exciting extension of our partnership and we look forward to hosting some Namibian teachers in Alsager in May 2005, when the African teachers arrive here".

David Black packing a box of useful items for our partner school in Oshilemba, Namibia.

By 1st September 2004, Alsager School had become a Business and Enterprise College (BEC). In other words, the school had become caught up in the all-encompassing 'specialist schools initiative'. This was a government initiative which had its origins, like many others, way back in the 1988 Education Reform Act. It encouraged secondary schools in England, to specialise in certain areas of the curriculum, to boost achievement. The initiative gained so much momentum, that by the time the scheme ended in 2010, there were nearly 3,000 specialist schools, which was fully 88% of the state-funded secondary schools in England.

To apply for specialist status, a school had to demonstrate reasonable standards of achievement, and produce a four-year development plan, with quantified targets related to learning outcomes. It also had to raise £50,000 (this amount was initially set at £100,000) in private sector sponsorship. Private sector sponsorship included charitable trusts, internal fund raising and donations from private companies. In some cases donations could be made in the form of goods or services.

Specialist schools still had to meet the full requirements of the English national curriculum, so the specialism was seen as adding value to the existing statutory provision rather than being a radical departure from it.

The requirement of raising sponsorship of £50,000 was considerable for many schools, so what was the financial incentive in return? The reward for achieving specialist status was a government grant of £100,000, to go with the £50,000 in sponsorship, for a capital project related to the specialism. There was also an additional £129 per pupil, per year for four years, to support the development plan.

The original specialism was Technology, which came on board in 1994, quickly followed by Languages, Arts and Sport in 1996. Business and Enterprise, Science, Engineering, Maths and Computing followed in 2001. A school could specialise in any one of the fields, or combine specialisms in two of them (at the same level of funding)

At Alsager, the green light for the planning and preparation for Business and Enterprise Status was given back in February 2003. Between then and September 2004, an enormous amount of work was done by the Senior Leadership Team, Business Studies, ICT and Maths staff to get everything ready for the final submission. Business and Enterprise was chosen as the specialism, as it was felt that the skills and aptitudes mentioned below, permeated the whole curriculum and were some of the most important attributes for young people to be successful, in an enterprising world of work.

The school even had a newly designed BEC logo, which appeared on all Alsager School signs and notepaper.

At the outset, all staff, pupils and parents needed to be made aware of the key purpose of a Business and Enterprise College and what 'Enterprise' actually meant. The school's 'shorthand' definition of Enterprise was that students are developing Enterprise skills, when they are engaged in:-

- Creative thinking
- Taking personal initiative
- Using presentational skills
- Developing self-confidence
- Team working
- Problem solving

Curriculum developments over the following years therefore focused on these skills and attributes, but the specific impact on the KS4 curriculum was to be as follows:

- Smaller classes in the three BEC subjects- Business and Communications Systems, ICT and Maths.
- All students had to achieve a qualification in ICT by the end of Year 10.
- Students would be offered the opportunity to study an additional GCSE in 'twilight' lessons.
- Accelerating some students, so that they took some GCSEs at the end of Year 10.
- All students had to study one subject which had a BEC focus.
- Enterprise activities were introduced into the KS3 curriculum eg the focus of 'Challenge' week changed to become 'Enterprise' week. This was the forerunner of PINC and SPIRIT.

Another example of how the BEC funding was used to good effect, was in the creation of a 'state of the art' multi-media language laboratory that completely enhanced the teaching and learning of modern foreign languages. It allowed students to work independently, using a variety of audio and visual materials. The

Modern Languages Laboratory was named after Deputy Head and linguist, Hedley Austen, who had recently retired.

The specialist schools programme, like most government initiatives was transient. When Mr Cameron's Coalition government took power in May 2010, the scheme was ended and funding was absorbed into general schools' budget.

Autumn 2007 saw Alsager School gain further national recognition by achieving the Inclusion Quality Mark (IQM). In the years prior to this, a large proportion of Government legislation, most notably 'Every Child Matters' and the Children's Act 2004, not to mention the OFSTED framework of the time, highlighted the importance of creating more inclusive schools. Indeed, 'inclusion' was one of the main 'buzz' words of the second half of the decade. However, unlike much of the jargon that was being pushed around, it related to a foundation on which all schools should be built.

At Alsager School, there was and still is, a strong belief that young people are genuinely included, when:

"They have full access to the school's social, extra-curricular and academic life. They will experience a welcome and acceptance, as well as real friendship, positive relationships and learning experiences, which are both challenging and personally satisfying".

Of course, this is the essence of our long standing mission statement 'An achieving school: a caring community' and it was with this in mind that the school set about the very rigorous process of fulfilling the 10 aspects of inclusive practice within the IQM. It really was a 'Heineken' experience, an evaluation of the school's processes and procedures which other evaluations do not reach. It was all pervading and took a great deal of worthwhile effort.

In July 2007 the School was extremely fortunate to receive donations from three incredibly generous parent-sponsors and life-long supporters of the school - Barry and Rosemary Leese, Mike and Sandra Moors and Peter Coates. With the Gift Aid the school

Carey Willetts from the band 'Athlete' who opened the Jill Bristow Performing Arts Centre.

was able to claim back from HMRC, the total sponsorship amounted to £250,000, which was put into a 'building futures' fund. With the agreement of the sponsors, this fund was allowed to accumulate for a number of years as it was ear-marked for a particular project. These donations, supplemented by £700,000 from Cheshire East and some money from school funds, eventually payed for the building of a new 'state of the art' Performing Arts Centre, which opened in 2011. It was named in memory of the late Jill Bristow, who had so much involvement with the fund raising and planning. I think she would have been delighted with and very proud of the new Centre. The actual opening ceremony was performed by musician, singer, song writer, Carey Willetts, from the band 'Athlete' and an impressive, former 'A' Level Geography student of mine.

On 22nd July 2007, I retired after 29 years at Alsager School. I was given a wonderful send off, both in the staff room and at the Chimney House Hotel, Sandbach. The fact that so many past and present colleagues attended the evening event made it a very emotional experience. I was chauffeured from my home by a parent who worked for Bentley. He brought a vintage motor and we went to the hotel via Congleton, so he could put the car through its paces along the A34. A real experience for which I was most grateful. I am also grateful to Jenny Broad who organised the evening so beautifully.

I had some lovely letters on the evening, even one from Ed Balls MP, the then Secretary of State for Education and more latterly 'Strictly'

The entrance to the JB Performing Arts Centre.

super star. There was also a teaching award, signed by Shirley Williams or Baroness Williams of Crosby. Not quite Nat Lofthouse but it was a pleasant surprise.

Of course, I had to make a nerve-racking speech, so started by telling everyone how homesick I was when I first moved to Alsager, all those years ago. So much so, that after a month I went to Dr Minns, my GP, for help.

> I said "Doctor my homesickness is so bad I can't stop singing
> The Green Green Grass of Home".
> He said "Sounds like Tom Jones syndrome to me, Lindsay".
> "Is that common doctor", I asked.
> "It's Not Unusual", he replied.

I loved that Tommy Cooper joke!

The worst part of retiring was clearing out my office during the penultimate week of term. It seemed as if my life's work was

My retirement do with Jane Griffiths, Nicky James, Jane Hamilton and Pam Hamilton.

David Black giving a speech at my retirement do.

disappearing before my eyes. I was always a hoarder and kept lots of old photos, videos, DVDs and documents etc. that went way back in the annals of time. Nobody wanted my piece of history, so I am sad to say much of it was thrown away. I could really have done with some of it now, to help with the writing of my story!

As the only secondary school in the Town, Alsager School had always benefited from excellent relationships with its partner primary schools. Traditionally they had always been Alsager Highfields, Cranberry, Pikemere, Excalibur, Rode Heath, Church Lawton Gate and St Gabriels Roman Catholic Primary. In terms of the latter, Catholic pupils should have attended St Thomas Moore in Crewe, which some did, but more recently it is true to say, larger numbers began to stay in Alsager for their secondary education. Church Lawton Gate closed its doors as a community primary school in July 2009 because of falling rolls.

Although, these schools always met regularly and worked closely in partnership, in 2009, under the guidance and drive of Mr Black, the Heads decided to create a much more formal arrangement of collaborative working. 'Alsager Community Trust' (ACT) was born! The newly formed Trust was registered under the Companies Act of 2006, the Schools in the Trust became Foundation, rather than Community Schools and were governed by legally documented 'Articles of Association' and a Board of Trustees. Cranberry could only be an associate member of the Trust, as they had already become a member of the St Bartholomew's Academy Trust and likewise, St Gabriels, could only be an associate member, as they were a religious foundation school. Rode Heath chose not to join the Trust and stayed out of the partnership.

Creating the Trust was a far sighted and courageous initiative by Heads. The key to its long term success was willing co-operation and a real desire to share expertise. Equally, Heads were flexible and generous in the way they managed both financial and other resources. They viewed the work of the Trust in its entirety and made decisions accordingly.

To meet the increasing demands of 'partnership' work on the ACT budget, individual schools contributed up to a maximum of £25 per student. Additional external funds, to support specific projects, came from Cheshire East, Alsager Rotary, Alsager Round Table, Alsager Partnership, The Town Council, Alsager Educational Foundation, Alsager Lions Club, Beech Hall School Trust and the Co-op Community Fund. The partnership of schools was so grateful to these organisations for their generosity over the years.

The ACT annual programme of events for pupils made impressive reading each year. Such a programme could not be organised without input and drive from all areas of the partnership, with everyone striving hard to improve the education and support for our children and young people.

One of the most impressive programmes each year, and the one that parents are most aware of, has been the inter-schools sports and activities programme. This took place on a Thursday evening, straight after school, and seemed to cover 'every sport known to man' (or woman for that matter). It was organised over many years by Alsager School PE teachers - Pat Arnott, then Steph Moore and now Rob Morris, along with the Sports Co-ordinators from each of the Primary Schools, who gave up so much of their time and deserve our thanks.

David Black retired in August 2011 after 18 years in charge. During his time he very successfully steered the school through a period of significant change. When asked about these changes, he focused on one change in particular and made the following observation.

"ICT, in its different forms, progressively made its way into all classrooms. Indeed, if you went back 30 years and walked around Alsager School, it would be the absence of IT that would strike you most. Otherwise pupil-teacher interaction would be similar".

Mr Black made his 'Fond Farewell' to students and parents in the Summer edition of School Matters 2011. I have included some extracts.

David Black, his Fond Farewell.

"We have a brilliant staff at Alsager School and I would like to thank them for the positive difference they have made to so many young people.... I know they acknowledge how lucky they all are to work in a school like this and I will always look back with fond memories of the students here. The vast majority are decent young people, who will become a force for good in the world.... Naturally, I have mixed feelings about leaving but it has been made easier in that I am confident my successor, Richard Middlebrook, is a very fine appointment and will take the school on to even greater heights. I wish Alsager School and everyone in it, the very best for the future".

A number of events were arranged to celebrate David's retirement. The main one was a buffet for staff, past and present, in the Hollinshead Hall at school. Ian White, Chair of Governors, celebrated David's many achievements as Head, in his own inimitable style. A further evening was held at the Oriental Restaurant in Sandbach.

Chapter 7: A Melting Pot of External Influences

Not everything in education was positive during these times. As schools moved further into the eighties, school numbers began contracting, a consequence of changing fertility patterns in the late sixties and seventies, when the number of live births fell by 35% by 1977. This was certainly the case in Alsager, where many areas had ageing population profiles. In Cheshire, the primary school population continued to fall until as late as 1987, while the secondary population, from a peak in 1980 fell 29% by 1993.

This was also a period of national and global economic recession. Financial cut-backs became the order of the day, which made education difficult to administer, as a service. Local Authorities were forced into school closures, amalgamations and a re-examination of the principles by which schools were staffed and pupil intakes determined.

Heads had to negotiate redundancies, early retirements and redeployments. It forced a rationalisation of the internal management of the school, which in turn affected teaching and learning, through the changing framework of the curriculum

The pressures on Mr Andrews were great. On January 15th 1981 he wrote:

"Today I was told that I will be losing five staff for next September. -2 for falling rolls and -3 because of the new Cheshire policy. Congleton District is -11 staff because of the new policy. I shall have to cope but I must record my disgust at what I see as a vicious attack upon State Education".

Redeployment became a feature of education appointments in Cheshire, the County became 'ring fenced' to outside applicants and on 11th February 1981, all Alsager staff were given redeployment letters. At the start of the new school year, on September 15th 1981, Mr Andrews wrote:

"The school is operating under the most serious financial and staffing constraints. Hard times".

Also on the 15th September 1981, for the first time, Alsager School was required, to produce a School Brochure, which had to contain all the school's external examination results, so giving parents a benchmark of the school's success (certainly in the eyes of the Government.)

At the start of 1984 relations between the Government and teachers unions were at a low ebb, over the Burnham Committee's pay offer of 4.5%. Teacher's today may find this surprising, given the years of austerity they have had to endure.

Alsager School had to close at lunchtimes, as there was no lunch time supervision. No cover for absent colleagues, meant a radical re-think of arrangements for the school day and staffing the curriculum. There were also intermittent strikes. These challenges continued into 1985.

It is also noticeable throughout the seventies and eighties, how often Alsager School and other schools in Cheshire were closed because of inclement weather. Today this hardly ever happens but harsh winters were much more frequent and had a much greater impact on schools. On December 13th 1981 Mr Andrews writes:

"Bad day of blizzards. All Cheshire schools closed on Monday. Carol Service postponed. -29° at Shawbury".

1988 was a very significant year for Alsager Comprehensive School. It was the year of the Education Reform Act, which was the most far-reaching education act of parliament since the 1944 Act. Historically, however, central government first crossed the threshold into 'the secret garden of the school curriculum' in October 1976, when James Callaghan, the Labour Prime Minister, delivered his famous speech at Ruskin College, Oxford, to launch 'The Great Debate'. From this time on, government influence over the curriculum grew exponentially, leading up to the 1988 Act and the launch of a National Curriculum.

On 1st November 1988 Mr Andrews wrote:

"First copies of the Education Act 1988 and the DES Circulars on the Local Management of Schools were received in school".

Nothing was ever the same again!

ERA or the' Baker Act' as it became known, after Kenneth Baker, the Conservative Secretary of State for Education at the time, brought in the following changes:

- An element of choice, where parents could specify their preferred choice of secondary school.
- Key Stages, each with their own educational objectives.
- The National Curriculum.
- Grant Maintained Schools.
- City Technology Colleges, which were the fore-runners of today's Academies.
- Local Management of Schools, whereby schools were given the power to manage their own financial and other affairs, thereby removing considerable power from the Local Authorities and giving these powers to Heads and school Governing Bodies.

The Act was presented as giving power to the schools. It certainly took power away from the LEAs and gave hundreds of new powers to the Secretary of State. Schools did have more say over the management of their own financial and other affairs and the relationship between Heads and Governing Bodies, changed forever. Schools and Heads became much more accountable.

Some would say Margaret Thatcher took a public service and turned it into a market, something the Tories had been working towards for a decade.

"The 1988 Act was in many ways a tribute to the remarkable resilience of the comprehensive ideal. Having failed to get selection reinstated in 1979, the Tories now used devices like opting out of LA control, open admission, city technology colleges and the introduction of 'local markets' ... as attempts to introduce selection by the back door" (Chitty and Dunford 1988)

In 1997 Sir Ron Dearing published his report, commissioned by the Government, 'Higher Education in a Learning Society'. David Blunkett, the then Labour Secretary of State for Education, accepted its central recommendation to introduce university tuition fees. Surprisingly, at the time, to little dissent. The first fees were then introduced for those going to university in September 1998, which as luck would have it, was the year my son left Alsager School for university. Having seen the subsequent escalation in fees over the years, I now count myself lucky!

One of the most significant external influences on any school has got to be an OFSTED inspection and a history of any school would be incomplete without a mention of OSTED (The Office for Standards in Education).

OFSTED was actually formed under the Education (Schools) Act 1992, as part of the increasing centralisation of the school system which began in 1988 with the 'Baker Reforms'. It was in 1992, that the first Common Inspection Framework was created and the first actual school inspections took place in September 1993.

Before this time, there was Her Majesty's Inspectorate of Schools (HMI). A 'lofty', politically independent organisation of experienced and well respected professionals, which dated back to 1839, well before the DFE was even thought of. Its role was/is:

- to advise the Secretary of State
- to preserve the quality of education in schools
- to provide a professional view on the quality of education with particular emphasis on the curriculum.

Since the inception of OFSTED, Alsager School has had four inspections. Our first experience was on 18th November 1996 and would you believe, there was a blizzard. Most Cheshire schools were shut but we carried on regardless. About 80% of our pupils made it, many in 'dribs and drabs' during the morning. Just what we wanted! But OFSTED were impressed with the efficient way in which the school kept running and the sensible behaviour of our students.

Suffice to say, the inspection was a very different beast to today's experience. The school had about six weeks' notice and was expected to gather an enormous quantity of information, relating to every aspect of school life. Being particularly conscientious and eager to please, we went completely over the top. I have vivid recollections of the floor of Mr Black's study, covered with large boxes full of files, all waiting to be sent off to the chief inspector, Mrs Kaye. Did she read all of this material? Who knows? I doubt it very much.

Mr Black's Study covered with boxes.

On the day, sixteen inspectors, having braved the snowy conditions, arrived at 8.00 am. A member of staff reported that she had seen one inspector hiding in the cleaner's cupboard, on the bottom floor of the Parker Building, presumably to see how well the students moved along our narrow corridors. The students were marvellous throughout and even curbed their exuberance for snowball fights at break and lunchtimes. Inspectors were there for the week and observed 245 lessons. It was a thoroughly exhausting experience. Every teacher was observed between two and five times and all these lessons were graded 1-7. Those who had top (1) grades were presented with certificates. All very competitive! Morale and team spirit were Churchillian.

In the end, we were graded 'very good'. We missed the 'excellent' grade by a 'whisker' and believe it or not we were a little disappointed.

"Alsager School is a very good school. The quality of teaching is markedly good and pupils achieve well and make good progress within a caring and secure framework....Moral education is a strong feature of the school. Pupils have a clear sense of right and wrong... At no time during the inspection was inappropriate behaviour observed. The Head provides clear leadership and vision and is well supported by experienced and dedicated deputy heads".

Later OFSTED frameworks removed the very good category and today, of course, we have 'outstanding' and 'good' as the two top grades.

The next inspection was in November 2001 and again we failed narrowly to get the top grade. By this time we had to settle for 'Good', with some outstanding features. The OFSTED team identified two areas for improvement and I hope you have a wry smile on your faces, when you read them.

1. Statutory requirements for a daily act of collective worship and for religious education in the Sixth Form are not met.

2. Provision for spiritual development is unsatisfactory.

For the most part, the school did act on these recommendations. For instance, it reviewed its policy on the daily act of collective worship. It also wrote to the Secretary of State, pointing out that post-16 students in FE Colleges were not required to study RE and that this particular post-16 curriculum requirement should be harmonised across the sectors. The school also asked the Cheshire adviser for RE to visit, to explain the difference between Religious Education and Spiritual Education. Not enough 'awe and wonder' still springs to mind, as part of the response! I also seem to remember this going down like a 'lead balloon' with staff, following a day's training on Spiritual Education! Now, whenever, I am on top of a peak in the Alps, taking in the view, before skiing off, I invariably think 'awe and wonder'. That OFSTED experience is with me for life.

By the time of the third inspection, in late September 2009, there had been a complete change of focus in terms of the framework. Schools were now only being given three days' notice of the inspection and asked to complete their own Self-evaluation of their progress. On the days of the inspection, we were visited by a small team and again the judgement was - 'Alsager is a Good School'. One of the most pleasing outcomes was the identification of the fact that:

"Alsager did as well for the least able students in the school, as it did for the most able".

The final OFSTED Inspection was on 2-3rd February 2016. A far more sensible streamlined process with no notice, just a phone call the day before, only three inspectors and only a very small amount of documentation to submit. The 'Overall Effectiveness' of the school was judged to be 'Outstanding'. A relatively small percentage of schools gain this outstanding badge, which makes it an even more prestigious achievement. At last we had made it, the OFSTED top grade! Alsager School does not work towards OFSTED success, as there are far more important goals, but nevertheless an amazing achievement for everyone, of which they should be very proud.

There were just a few findings which stood out for me:

"Outstanding leadership at all levels is a hallmark of the school".

"There is a strong sense of collective responsibility. Pride in the school is shared by staff, governors, pupils and their families".

"The very high standard of teaching leads to pupils making outstanding progress".

"The welfare and personal development of pupils is a very high priority for all staff".

Anyone involved in teaching at the start of 2003, will never forget the impact on the profession of 'Raising Standards and Tackling Workload: a National Agreement'. This was an historic agreement, whereby the Government and employers accepted the union position that teachers should not have to undertake administrative roles. Fundamentally, 'workforce reform' grew out of the conviction that:

"The school workforce is key to raising standards of achievement and that teachers need to be free of tasks which are not concerned with their core job of teaching, if they are to help children and young people realise their potential".

Firstly, the agreement stated that teachers should not routinely do administrative and clerical tasks, which should be done by support staff. Such tasks included, collecting money, chasing absences bulk photocopying, classroom displays, processing exam results, collating pupil reports, administering and invigilating examinations, stocktaking, data analysis, to mention a few.

Secondly, Governing Bodies had to ensure that Heads had an appropriate workload, in support of a reasonable work/life balance, having regard to their health and welfare. Equally, headteachers needed to ensure that their staff were afforded the same support, in terms of workload and work/life balance.

Thirdly there were to be limits on the extent to which teachers at the school could be asked to cover unexpectedly for absent colleagues, with the progressive movement towards a position where this should happen only rarely. Initially, the number of cover hours per year was set at 38, but actual numbers should have been well below this maximum. The time scale for implementing these changes was relatively short and many of the changes had to be in place for September 2003. Others of course, would need more time to implement.

The impact on Alsager and other schools was far reaching, though in many respects Alsager was ahead of the game. Mr Black had already put in place an extremely well developed support staff structure, which was better placed to pick up many of these tasks than a great number of other schools. Nevertheless, it was not an easy time for the school.

Although the general principles of the national agreement were laudable in many respects, Alsager already had a number of school-based agreements in place, which related to improving teacher workload and work/life balance. This national/local trade off caused conflict at times with some of the unions, who seemed a little intransigent in their approach. This is, of course, a personal opinion and one that some staff would reject.

Today's school landscape, in which we see independent invigilators, supply teacher recruitment agencies, cover supervisors and an army of support staff, can be traced back, in the main, to this national agreement on workforce reform. Interestingly, when I arrived at Alsager Comprehensive School in 1978, there were 1700 pupils in the school, a bursar, Barbara Meddings, and just 3 secretaries. Hilda Howard, was Mr Andrews' secretary and June Ozanne and Judy Parrish, both worked in the main office.

Also from around 2003, there was a huge drive towards more effective 'safeguarding' of our young people. Safeguarding is a concept that reaches beyond child protection, even though the phrases are often used interchangeably. The former designated Safeguarding Lead at school, Ellen Walton, once told me that:

'If safeguarding can be thought of as a filing cabinet, then child protection is simply one draw'.

Each year, all staff and governors are given a booklet from the DFE, called 'Keeping Children Safe in Education', which they are expected to sign, to confirm it has been read. This document outlines their statutory duties, to safeguard and promote the welfare of children. It defines safeguarding as:

- Protecting children from maltreatment.
- Preventing impairment of children's health and development.
- Ensuring children grow up in circumstances consistent with the provision of safe and effective care.
- Taking action to enable all children to have the best outcomes.

This, as you can imagine, has become a huge responsibility for schools and the staff who work in them.

So why this shift, from traditional child protection, to a more all-encompassing approach? The origins go back to a Safeguarding Children's report in 2002 and the high profile, Victoria Climbié Inquiry of 2003. Out of the latter came the 'Every Child Matters' framework, outlined in the Children Act 2004. This was regarded as one of the most important policy initiatives ever introduced in relation to the children and families agenda. ECM aimed to improve outcomes for children in 5 key areas.

- Being healthy
- Staying safe
- Enjoying and achieving
- Making a positive contribution
- Achieving economic well-being

It was an agenda schools could realistically work with and certainly fired the imagination of the pastoral staff at Alsager School. Certain aspects of ECM dovetailed into the school becoming a Business and Enterprise College in 2004 and it was the corner stone of the school's bid to gain the Inclusion Quality Mark, in 2007.

However, since the Cameron Government in 2010, there has been a move away from the ECM terminology and funding has been deflected towards different approaches. The Government has released a number of updated versions of the document 'Working Together to Safeguard Children', which sets out ways in which organisations and individuals should work together to safeguard and promote the well-being of children.

The impact of all this legislation on Alsager School was and is huge. The role of the designated Safeguard Lead, currently Adele Snape, one of the Deputy Heads, and the College Managers, is enormous, as is the level of responsibility. I am the Safeguard Governor and I meet with the Deputy Head, on a regular basis, to keep abreast of developments. In a recent communication, I was astonished by the scale of interaction between those involved with safeguarding responsibilities at school and vulnerable families and this was during the coronavirus 'lockdown period'. I thought it was a great testament to the school's mission statement - 'a caring community' and it made me feel proud to be part of such a community.

September 2007 was to have quite an impact on the teachers at Alsager School and on the profession as a whole. The Training and Development Agency for Schools (TDA) introduced a National Framework of Professional Standards for Teachers, at each career stage. For the first time, teachers advancing through each of these stages, would need to be assessed through an external assessment process and could only advance to the next stage, subject to satisfactory performance across a range of standards.

If they were eligible to advance to the 'halcyon' levels of Upper Pay Scales, they would have to go through the elusive 'threshold'. In the first few years when the threshold was introduced, thousands of teachers around the country spent an inordinate amount of time gathering huge amounts of evidence, to prove that they had indeed met the exacting standards to take them through to the higher pay grades. The teaching profession finally had its eyes opened to the joys of Performance Management and its impact on pay progression. Alsager School currently has a Performance Management process which is not only very rigorous but far more streamlined than those early systems outlined above. It applies to everyone from the Executive Head, to the most newly qualified teacher.

In October 1992 Jim Andrews recorded in his Headteacher's Log that two Cheshire Advisers, Mr Davice and Mr Williams were coming into school, to 'appraise' his performance as Headteacher. On March 2nd 1992 he comments that:

"Deputy Head appraisals begin this week".

Followed on March 23rd by:

"Data collected for Mr Purcell's appraisal and report written".

Little did we know then, how central Performance Management was going to become to the professional life of teachers at Alsager and other schools and how teachers increasingly would be held to account, in various ways, for their performance. I certainly can't remember what Jim Andrew's said to me in my appraisal but what I do know is that it didn't have any bearing on my pay grade.

Personally, I believe greater accountability is a good thing and can only improve the quality of learning in a school. Just as Governors hold the Head and Senior Leadership Team to account, so too should teachers be held to account in the quest for quality first, imaginative teaching.

I have mentioned the ever increasing impact of information technology and more recently the growing influence of safeguarding measures on Alsager School. To these, I must add a third and refer the reader back to crossing the threshold, into what was 'the secret garden of the school curriculum'. In other words, government influence, cynics would say interference, over what should be taught. Some examples, illustrate this point.

You will remember how the Education Reform Act 1988, introduced the National Curriculum, with its prescribed programmes of study and 10 levels of progression, over 4 Key Stages. It also introduced a new compulsory subject, Technology. This was prescription on a previously unprecedented level and, although greater flexibility was introduced into the later programmes of study, it marked a fundamental change to the approach of central government.

We have also seen how Alsager School in 2004 became a Specialist School. At that time, schools were told that the Specialist Schools Programme was a government initiative to encourage schools in England to specialise in certain areas of the curriculum, to 'boost achievement'. These specialisms, as we now know, included Engineering, Technology, Sports, Music and Arts (Performing, Visual and Media). Alsager chose Business and Enterprise, because it was felt this specialism offered a broader, cross-curricular base to students and in particular enterprise skills, which were fundamental to success in an adult world.

Fast forward to 2010. David Cameron's Coalition Government, with Michael Gove, Secretary of State for Education, introduced the concept of the English Baccalaureate (the EBacc). This is a school performance indicator linked to GCSE. It is not a qualification in itself. It measures the proportion of young people who secure a grade 5 (new GCSE grading system, also introduced as part of the recent GCSE reforms) or above in English, Maths, Science, a Humanities subject and a Modern Foreign Language GCSE.

The Government's intention in promoting this particular, more traditional, combination of subjects, was to ensure that all 16 year olds left school with a set of academic qualifications, which would improve their life chances and social mobility. It would also combat the perceived fall in the number of students studying foreign languages and science. (If only we knew where the language teachers were going to come from?)

It is fair to say that the EBacc has caused significant reaction and discussion at Alsager School and beyond. Essentially there has been extensive debate as to whether:

- the school believes that the whole concept of EBacc is best suited to the needs of our students and the validity on which the government premise is based.
- the school should spend its limited resources on incentivising the EBacc subjects, to achieve government targets or on subjects that may be more suitable for all of our students.

There is little doubt that across the country, the introduction of EBacc, has had a detrimental impact on the uptake of non-EBacc subjects. Following the 2019 GCSE results, for instance, there was a good deal of concern expressed in some quarters that the future for creative subjects was 'bleak'. There were also large decreases in individual subjects such as Design and Technology (23%) and PE (7.3%). The problem with subjects like Music and D&T are that they are expensive to run, and become even more expensive when there are fewer students in classes. It becomes easy to justify not running these classes on small numbers and looking to the future, if state schools are not mindful, these subjects may reside only with the independent schools.

And now for the good news! Schools like Alsager, have thrived on Music, Art, Drama, Sport and D&T and would never let these subjects disappear from the curriculum. There is so much evidence in this book, to show the talents of Alsager's young people in these subjects. They must be maintained at all costs.

So in summary, in a relatively short space of time, the DFE has moved from an emphasis on more practical, technological and vocational subjects, in its specialist schools programme, to a focus on more traditional academic subjects. Apparently, this is now the key to successful life chances and social mobility! Does this mean there has been a fundamental shift in the thinking of our most highly regarded educationalists? Or is it simply a question of political dogma and the fact that since 1971, there have been twenty two Secretaries of State for Education and only four have been in office long enough to see a fourth year - Margaret Thatcher, Sir Keith Joseph, David Blunkett and Mr EBacc himself, Michael Gove? I will leave you to be the judge of this.

What is certain though, is that those responsible for planning the curriculum in any school, should never move far away from the age-old mantra, that the curriculum should be 'broad and balanced', catering for a 'comprehensive' intake.

Chapter 8: The Sixth Form

Since it became a comprehensive school in 1971, Alsager School has educated the young people of the Town from the ages of 11-18 years. I have always been a great advocate of 11-18 schools and when I was looking for my next career move in 1978, I was only looking at schools with sixth forms. A sixth form brings so much benefit to a school as a whole, and for Alsager, its large Sixth Form has always been the 'jewel in the crown'.

So why was and is our Sixth Form so important? Teachers who teach across all Key Stages have the broader view of how learning fits together. They are able to ensure that the programmes of study in the main school, allow the students to cope with 'A Level' study. Post-16 transition can be disruptive to education, but this has not been the case at Alsager. For the most part, students know their teachers going into the sixth form, which makes the settling in process easier and encourages an early rapport between teachers and students.

Alsager School Upper Sixth 2000.

Our Sixth Form made teacher recruitment and retention easier, so there was a greater likelihood of the school having more specialist teachers, particularly in subjects like Maths, Physics and Chemistry.

Having older and younger students in the same school, where they could interact relatively easily, built a successful community. It offered sixth form students the opportunity to play a supporting role with younger students. They functioned as role models and could be inspirational for lower school students, especially in subjects like sport, drama, art and music. This high level of interaction, between older and younger students, has never been greater since the creation of the Colleges, the College Councils and the Sixth Form Student Management Team, led by our Head Boys and Girls. This Team was first created in 2010-11 and since that time Head Boys and Girls have included:

2010-11 - Tom Holdcroft and Georgette Brookes

2011-12 - James Newman and Kate Bryan

2012-13 - Matthew Swift and Kelly Quinn

2013-14 - Ryan Roman and Maisie Gittins

2014-15 - Joe Kelly and Olivia Cork

2015-16 - Martin Snewin and Ruth Newman

2016-17 - Callum Astley and Robyn Spiby

2017-18 - George Flanders and Charlotte Armstrong

2018-19 - Jakob Harper and Erika Levett

2019-20 - Shay Norman and Simone Spiby

As with most things in life and in education, great benefits usually come with a cost. I have described our Sixth Form as the 'jewel in the crown' and truly it was and still is to this day. But over the years, the Sixth Form has raised a number of significant philosophical and financial issues, for Senior Management Teams and Governors.

First Sixth Form Student Leadership Team.

In theory, since 1971, Alsager School has provided education for young people between the ages of 11-18 but in reality, for most of that time, the Sixth Form catered only for those young people best suited to 'A' Level courses. It was only in recent years that the curriculum diversified somewhat, to offer a more vocational diet. That is not to say curriculum diversity and the idea of a more 'open' sixth form was not discussed on a good many occasions, going back in time.

One such occasion was early 1996. Sir Ron Dearing had just finished his review of Post-16 Education, in which he proposed to rationalise the various courses and qualifications on offer. A central strand to this debate concerned 'A' Levels and General National Vocational Qualifications (GNVQ). Most people had a good appreciation of 'A' Level courses, which were and still are academic in nature. They build upon the study of many of the traditional subjects taken at GCSE. Although other subjects, not studied for GCSE, for example, Psychology, Sociology and Politics, had come on board by this time.

GNVQs, on the other hand, were broad-based vocational qualifications, relating to occupational areas. For example, GNVQ Performing Arts concentrated on practical matters relating to work in a theatre - props lighting, front of house etc -, while 'A

Level Theatre Studies, although touching on these practical areas, contained significant academic study, relating to reviews of plays and productions.

Assessment was also very different. GNVQ contained significant continuous assessment and was based on a 'competency' approach, while 'A Level was based on a more traditional terminal examination. GNVQs at this level were equivalent to two 'A' Levels. They were not easier than 'A' Levels but were better suited to some students.

Our School Governors debated at length, whether or not to introduce a limited range of GNVQs, which philosophically would have gone a long way to make Alsager School fully comprehensive and more inclusive up to the age of 18 years.

There were a number of reasons why they chose not to do so at the time.

Firstly, students in Year 11 went on to study a very wide range of GNVQs at the local colleges. Business Studies was the most popular GNVQ but only 9 of our students expressed an interest in it. It would not have been financially viable to run a course for only 9 students, let alone smaller numbers in other subjects. Also some of these students wanted to go to the colleges, rather than stay on at school, reducing the numbers further.

Secondly, former students who wanted to do GNVQs, were very well catered for by the colleges in Stoke, Newcastle, South Cheshire and Reaseheath. These all had excellent practical facilities for the courses and were within easy reach. The philosophical argument that our community school should 'provide for all' broke down somewhat, when excellent provision existed within the locality. Basically we could not compete effectively.

Finally, there were more practical matters. The school was full and it lacked the specialist accommodation, required to teach 20 or so GNVQ students.

In the end, the interests of the young people had to come first and Governors felt they would be better off attending one of the colleges, where the facilities and experience were readily available. Equally, 'A' Levels were one of Alsager School's strengths and the school should concentrate on this unrivalled provision.

Mrs Jackie Latham with one of her Year 13 Psychology Groups 2014.

I should point out that Alsager School now has a much broader post-16 provision and its Sixth Form is open to a much wider range of students but more on this curriculum debate in Chapter 10.

For the record the last GNVQs were awarded in 2007.

Further post-16 curriculum reforms were thrust upon the school in 1999 in the shape of Advanced Supplementary Level (AS level). This was intended to widen the range of subjects studied by 'A' Level students. The intention was that students would study 4 AS Levels in the Lower Sixth (Yr 12), continuing with two or three of these in the Upper Sixth to 'A' Level standard.

The position for Alsager students was rather different than in many other schools, because most of our students always studied four subjects in both the lower and upper sixth, i:e three specific subjects plus General Studies. General Studies was always considered to be important, because of the breadth of study it covered, including; Science, Maths, Modern Languages, Current Affairs and Politics, RE and Morals and Cultural Studies.

The irony for the school was that moving to the AS pattern was likely to narrow the range of study rather than broaden it. The school also had concerns about the demands that AS would place on our students, who would be taught for 38 out of 50 periods per fortnight. This was before any time was allocated to PE, Young Enterprise, Key Skills or any 'enrichment study'. All this left far less time for independent study and increased the homework load. For these reasons the school did not follow the AS pattern in its first year.

Each year, Year 13 always put considerable effort into raising money for charitable causes which the students decided to support. 1995 was a memorable year in this respect, as students set themselves an admirable target of £5000 which would go to the Roy Castle 'Cause for Hope' Appeal. The charity aimed to build the world's first hospital and research centre dedicated purely to lung cancer. Before he died, Roy Castle, the famous musician and entertainer did a great deal to raise money for this charity and the organisers decided to put his name to the centre.

The first fund raising event took place early in November when 40 Sixth Form students completed a 28 mile sponsored walk, from Manchester's Christie Hospital back to Rode Heath, raising a staggering £2000. Mr Plant, Head of Sixth Form said at the time:

"I will always remember the beautiful Autumn day, cheerful determination, not to mention the endless supply of blister-plasters, but most of all the phenomenal amounts of money that rolled in on the days that followed".

Sixth Form Students with cheque for the Roy Castle 'Cause for Hope' Appeal

With all the other activities that took place during the year, the students more than met their target and raised £5724.92 for the Roy Castle centre.

2001 was another year to highlight, in terms of Sixth Form Charity fund raising, as Year 13 raised £4,363 for Horton Lodge Special School, in Rudyard. Fund raising activities were varied, culminating in a sponsored walk from Alsager to Rudyard in July.

Throughout all the years of post-16 provision, there was always a Director of Sixth Form and in more recent times, as the size of the sixth form increased, a Deputy Director. They led a specialised team of form tutors, carefully monitored student progress and managed a multitude of procedures relating to developing links with universities, career and university applications and general student welfare.

Students receiving their 'A' Level results.

The 'pastoral care' side of Sixth Form provision has always been a great strength and identified as such by OFSTED, where they referred to the *"wrap around care"* that each student enjoys. Other aspects of the non-academic side of Sixth Form life which I particularly enjoyed were the presentation of awards events and the wonderful Sixth Form Balls, which seemed to be the only occasion at which I got to wear my tux!

The Director and Deputy's role was and still is a considerably demanding one but it has always been carried out with great professionalism and skill. Directors and Deputy Directors over the Years included:

Reverend John Hughes, Keith Plant, Jackie Latham, Joanne Williams, Andrew Wishart, Alison Pole and Andrew Evans. They have been very ably supported in recent years by Sixth Form Administrators Helen Barton and Clare Pass.

Mrs Christine Richards with her Upper Sixth Form 2000.

Staff at one of the splendid Sixth Form Leaving Balls.

Chapter 9: Education and Fun Beyond the Classroom

Even before the opening of the comprehensive school, trips in this country and abroad were a regular feature of school life. Many were activity holidays, many curriculum-related but whatever the purpose, they were all great fun for both students and staff and, I hope, packed full of life-long memories. I was fortunate to be involved in some of these trips and I can only say that they were wonderful experiences. It is impossible to mention them all but a small selection are mentioned within this chapter.

One of the earliest I encountered in the archives was a trip to Interlaken, Switzerland. It left Crewe station at 8.55 am on Thursday 6th June 1963, on the first leg of the journey to Euston. From there the party travelled by boat and overnight train to Basel and then on to Interlaken to stay at the City Hotel. The cost of the trip was £22 10s 3d in old money, of course. Quite a substantial sum in those days! Literally the high point of the trip was the ascent of the Jungfrau, (11,723 ft) from Grindelwald, which ultimately climbed on a railway through the North Face of the Eiger. The photograph below shows the students in the Ice Palace on the mountain.

Alsager Secondary School students in the Ice Palace on the Jungfrau.

In the Summer holiday of 1981 there were school trips to Brittany and Italy, a 10 day walking trip following the Pennine Way, which I joined for some of the time, and a sailing trip around the Hebrides. In addition, there were the annual French and German exchanges with schools in Brive and Reinbeck respectively.

The first French Exchange with Brive in the Dordogne in 1980.

November 1981 saw the first Sixth Form weekend to the Cheshire Centre at Menai on Anglesey. The chosen theme was 'Freedom and Authority'. This was followed by Energy in 1982.

On October 15th 1982, 70 first year students and staff went on an outdoor pursuits weekend to Grange over Sands. Each year Mr Steve Marshall organised these long weekend adventures for Year 7, to field centres around the North West and Midland areas.

On December 17th 1982, 20 pupils went with Mrs Needham and Mr Macpherson on a cruise on the SS Uganda to the Holy Land. Sadly, this was the last cruise voyage of the Uganda, as she was then requisitioned as a troopship for the Falklands War.

At Easter 1994, Mr Colin Jenkins from the History Department 'went boldly where no school trip had been before'. He organised an exchange with a school in Russia. A party of seven intrepid Sixth Form History and Politics students and Mr Jenkins made the long journey to Balacovo, a town 500 miles South East of Moscow. The students were Vicky Constantine, Lynn Jones, Karen Grinney, Clara Howell, Steven Micklewright, Stephen Moors and Alison Williams.

The reciprocal exchange took place the following July, when nine Russian students and two teachers stayed with their Alsager partners and some additional helpers - Lucie Broad, Matthew Wilson and Julie Davies. Most of our guests had never been outside Russia before and none of them had been to the 'West'. They were taken aback by western abundance and were first impressed by our motorway toilets. On arriving in Alsager, a huge gasp went up, when passing the greengrocer's shop in the school minibus and the 'hole in the wall' at Bank Corner gave further excitement. Not only did our guests sample the delights of Alsager but they also visited Alton Towers, London (including the Houses of Parliament), Nantwich and the Wedgewood factory. The students commented:

"Meeting the Russians and visiting their country has made us appreciate how much people in Britain take for granted".

A Selection of Photos of International School Trips

Students on a trip to Italy 1988.

Sixth Form History trip to Prague.

Sixth Form History Trip to New York and Washington. In front of the Manhattan Skyline.

First World War Battlefields Trip 17th-19th July 1999

In July 1999 Hedley Austen and I had the real pleasure of accompanying Mrs Jan Shaw and Ms Amanda Davies and forty two Year 10 students to the World War 1 Battlefields. Our Commander was Mrs Christine Routs, a formidable leader and long-time member of the Western Front Society. Our itinerary was meticulously planned and with Mrs Routs out front, her troops followed in very orderly fashion, not far behind.

Ferry Crossing to the Battlefields - Hedley Austen, Amanda Davies, Christine Routs, Jan Shaw.

We hit the beaches at Calais on Saturday 17th July and headed straight to our first engagement at Ypres (Ieper) Salient, Belgium, where we negotiated some very muddy, original trenches at Sanctuary Wood. From here we visited Langemarck, the only German cemetery in the Salient with 44,292 burials in multiple or mass graves.

Compared to the Allied cemeteries, Langemarck was dark, the headstones were flat to the ground and there was no birdsong. At the end of the day, the troops moved forward to the Menin Gate and the Last Post Ceremony, at 8.00 pm. By its very simplicity, this was one of the most moving experiences imaginable, standing

Students with Ieper Fire Service Buglers at Menin Gate Ceremony.

in silence beneath an impressive memorial, commemorating the 54,000 soldiers who gave their lives on the Ypres Salient, 1914-17 and who have no known grave.

Late that evening we eventually arrived at our billets. We were to be stationed at the Northern French town of Bethune. An early start and the 'big push' to the Somme Battlefield, South West of Bethune on the Sunday. The main Battle of the Somme was fought between July and November 1916 and in many ways was one of the greatest disasters ever experienced by the British Army. The troops were somewhat hesitant about the experiences that lay ahead.

The Somme, like Ypres, had its memorial to those soldiers who have no known grave. This stands at Thiepval and remembers

73,000 men whose names are inscribed on this vast edifice. Vimy Ridge, a short distance from the Somme proper, is a tribute to the sons of Canada who fought and died in trenches and shell holes, just a 'stone's throw' from the German fortifications. It also gave us some understanding of tunnel warfare. Newfoundland Park was one of the most moving sites, as on 1st July 1916 the untried Newfoundland Regiment, who paid their own passage across the Atlantic, were decimated by the intense and accurate machine gun fire of experienced German troops. In 1919, the Newfoundland Government acquired the area, as a permanent memorial to the sacrifice of its sons.

Perhaps, most moving of all, was Mansell Copse and the battle to take Fricourt. The 9th Devonshires had to cross South of Mametz, where the Germans had a machine gun strategically placed in the cemetery, behind a shrine. Both Captain Martin and Lieutenant Hodgson MC predicted that if the British bombardment had not silenced the German defences, then they and their men were doomed. Their predictions were accurate and the Devonshires were gunned down by the machine gun, as they advanced from Mansell Copse. Lieutenant Hodgson appears to have realised his imminent death, for two days before the attack he wrote a poem called Before Action, the moving, last verse of which appears below.

I, that on my familiar hill

Saw with uncomprehending eyes

A hundred of Thy sunsets spill

Their fresh and sanguine sacrifice,

Ere the sun swings his noonday sword

Must say goodbye to all of this:

By all delights that I shall miss,

Help me to die, O Lord.

At the end of the day, the Chaplain collected the bodies of the men and had them buried in their trench, in what is now known as Devonshire Cemetery. A board erected on the site records:

"The Devonshires Held This Trench, The Devonshires Hold It Still".

We visited many other very moving, yet uplifting, sites during a very full day. Christine Routs plotted her way around the Somme Battlefields with 'military precision'. That night back at our billet in Bethune, in spite of exhaustion, I found it difficult to sleep as there were so many emotions running wild around my head.

Day three saw our troop back at the Ypres Salient and a visit to Tyne Cot, the largest British War Cemetery in the world. In the Battle of Passchendaele, German pill boxes played a major role and the Northumberland Fusiliers saw in them a resemblance to Tyneside cottages, silhouetted on the horizon. This led to them calling them 'Tyne cottages' and hence the name Tyne Cot.

In all, 11,871 graves are registered in the cemetery, of which 70% are unidentified, witnesses in many cases to the horrifying strength of the vile Passchendaele mud which sucked into its morass a man and his means of identity. On the wall at the back of the cemetery are the names of 34,908 soldiers who have no known grave.

While at the cemetery, another school party entered this hallowed place. A boy was kicking a football around, the teacher striding forward, doing nothing, cup of tea in hand. Too much for our Commander who swiftly took action, delivering an on the spot 'court martial'. Boy and teacher immediately left the cemetery with ball and cup before returning in more respectful manner, suitably chastened. The reason I mention this is that, throughout the tour, our troops were remarkable in the levels of gravitas, sensitivity, respect and understanding that they demonstrated in a very emotionally charged environment. No more than I would have expected of Alsager School's young troops.

We ended the tour at the excellent 'In Flanders Fields Museum', housed in the Cloth Hall in the centre of Ypres, which gives a most realistic feeling of the horrors of the Great War. In my opinion, everyone should experience a visit to the First World War Battlefields. If one of the lead OFSTED inspectors wanted to see our young people experience 'the spiritual', then this was it! I was so moved by my experience with our students, that I returned with my wife the following October Half Term and, with minor modifications (a visit to the Welsh Memorial), followed the same itinerary.

A Geography first in the French Alps: June 1993

In October 1992 the Geography Department began to plan its annual 'A' Level residential fieldtrip. But this year was different. No more rainy, windswept, Welsh hillsides or storm bound Anglesey beaches, they were heading to the French Alps at the end of June 1993. Never before had the department received a single offer of help with fieldwork, from outside the Humanities Faculty, but suddenly Modern Language teachers felt their linguistic skills were needed. Scientists were sure that they too could bring invaluable assistance!

As June approached, excitement rose, especially amongst the staff who were to accompany the Lower Sixth students - Joyce Halsall, Sue Young and Philip Clarke. Six Upper Sixth geography students were to join the group, to widen their experience before embarking on their university courses.

The group set out one cool Saturday in June. The coach journey passed pleasantly, and bright sunshine greeted our geographers when they arrived in Villeneuve/Serre Chevalier. With no time to waste, the first piece of fieldwork was organised immediately after lunch on the Sunday. The environment was superb in the Romanche Valley, plants were in full flower, which made recognition relatively straight forward. Student questionnaires, in French of course, were completed efficiently and the hypotheses tested all proved correct.

However the high point of the week was the day spent on the Glacier Blanc. The one and a half hour trek up the mountain was

more than compensated for by the sheer scale and splendour of the glacier itself. The ice cave, at the base of the glacier's snout, was like walking into an aquamarine ice cube! The area was so breathtaking that the group spent the first thirty minutes simply absorbing the awe and wonder of it all.

By the end of the week, strong friendships had been formed and it was with great sadness that the school's Canadian exchange student, Jeff Burnett, prepared for his return home, soon after his return to Alsager.

'A Level' Geography Students under the snout of the Glacier Blanc.

It was no cliché to say that the whole group found the trip such a rewarding and worthwhile experience, and not one student complained about working until 9.30 pm each evening. It is also true to say that the geography department never looked back. Their horizons were certainly broadened in terms of future field trip venues, with excursions back into Europe and Iceland becoming the norm.

Adventure and Risk in the Great Outdoors

Arguably the greatest highlight of my teaching career at Alsager School was the time spent outside the classroom with the students. Much of this time was spent doing fairly challenging activities, often in mountainous areas. In those days teachers were not required to complete in depth risk assessments, they relied on common sense and experience. Alsager was blessed with a wealth of staff, who were well qualified and experienced mountain leaders, climbers, canoeists and sailors. The opportunities offered to students reflected these skills. These staff included Graham Shaw, Derek Brooks, Stella Spratley, Alan Danby, Ian Macpherson, Jim Wiltshier, Tessa Fenoughty, Dave Throp and Jim Andrews himself. The outdoor pursuits co-ordinator for many of these years was Steve Marshall. I learned a great deal from these staff by accompanying them on many trips.

At certain times of year, The Design Courtyard, now 'The Shack' café, was filled with canoes and sailing dinghies. One of these dinghies belonged to Jim Andrews. I am reliably told, but will not reveal my source, that someone engraved *"Jock"* (Mr Andrews' nickname) in the woodwork. This remained there for four years before being sanded out. There was also a store room, off the old Social Area (which became the 'Zest' cafe), filled with all sorts of camping equipment, life jackets, paddles, climbing helmets and other outdoor pursuits equipment for the student's use.

Each year, at the beginning of the Summer holidays, Ian Macpherson would lead a long distance walk with a group of our students, planned around Youth Hostels. Sometimes they would be linear walks with the school minibus in support - the Pennine Way or the Coast to Coast, at other times the walks would be circular, for instance around the Lake District or the Yorkshire Dales.

Deputy Head, Ian Macpherson, parent Jeff Sutton and a party of students complete the Pennine Way, Summer 1977.

All the walks were amazing experiences but the one that really stood out for me was my first. In the Summer of 1979 a group of 12 students, Ian Macpherson, Dave Bullock and I embarked on the 30 highest peaks of the Lake District in 6 days. It was a gruelling schedule, with two of the days being particularly demanding. I was 29 years of age and in quite good shape but still found it a challenge to keep up with some of the lads, who were like mountain goats. Indeed we resorted to slipping the odd rock or two in their rucksacks to slow them down. On day three, after two days of running down scree slopes, trying to keep up, my knee started to swell. Falling well off the pace and out of sight of the group when I finally made the road, I managed to persuade a kindly driver to give me a lift to the Youth Hostel. I slumped down in my seat, so no one could see me drive past and was waiting to greet my comrades who had walked the three miles along the road to the Wast Water Youth Hostel. I took some abuse for my underhand actions. The students on the trip were first rate in all respects and it was a pleasure to be with them. The weather was also astonishing for The Lakes. Bright sunshine throughout the week, lots of suntan cream and not a drop of rain falling on our rucksacks. Perfect!

Paddle Boarders on Astbury Mere, Congleton, during PINC Week

Parents and students will remember Challenge Week, which became Enterprise Week, which became PINC and then broadened into SPIRIT, during the Richard Middlebrook era. (More on SPIRIT later) These were the times when the timetable was suspended and students were engaged in all sorts of alternative 'enriching' activities.

My part in all this was to accompany our mountain leader, Mr Graham Shaw, to Snowdonia, where we would stay in a centrally placed Youth Hostel and each day our group would climb various peaks in the National Park. A favourite of ours was always the North Ridge of Tryfan, which, rather than being a long slog up a 3000 ft peak, is a grade 1 scramble. Much more interesting and challenging for our Year 9 students and an experience they would never forget. The students were all kitted out in helmets, staff had ropes, in case of an emergency and the ascent began from Llyn Ogwen. One ascent I will never forget is the one with Steven Garrett. Every 100 feet or so there would be this voice in my ear - *"Are we near the top yet Sir?"* *"No, not yet Steven. Dig in and keep climbing".* And so it went on. Eventually we reached the summit at just over 3000 feet, quite a peak with magnificent 360° views. Steven- *"Are we near the top yet Sir?"* With great disbelief in my tone, I replied *"Yes Steven, there is only The Lord above us now".*

In spite of numerous requests, we would never let any of the students jump between Adam and Eve, the two standing stones on the summit.

On another occasion, we were descending from Carnedd Llewelyn, the second highest mountain in England and Wales and arrived at a bridge, crossing a rocky gorge with a stream running through it. It was May and the weather was not particularly warm. There was some casual conversation about how good it would be to swim through the gorge if the weather was warmer. We were just about to walk off when there was an almighty splash. Looking around, Jonathan Broomhall had leapt into the gorge, in his shortsand was swimming under the bridge we were crossing. Everyone was cheering him on. It was a great moment as he emerged from the water at the far end of the gorge. From that time on he assumed hero status. Where was health and safety? You may well ask? I am sure the staff would have jumped in, should the need have arisen.

The third incident from these trips to North Wales which sticks firmly in my memory, is one that happened at the Dolgarrog Gorge in the Conwy Valley. In the early years of Challenge we would stop off here on the way to Snowdonia. Dolgarrog is a series of waterfalls running down the side of the Conwy Valley but the flow of the water has been diverted for HEP purposes. As a result, there is now only a trickle of water coming over the 'downfalls' but a number of fine 'plunge pools' at the bases. In short this makes an ideal location for climbing up the rock faces from one waterfall to the one above and then swimming in the plunge pools. The modern term for this activity I believe is canyoning.

Students out and about in Snowdonia.

For this the students, of course, wore helmets and were roped up while climbing the rock faces. The vast majority of young people loved doing this activity, particularly when their confidence started to increase. But on one occasion a student, while climbing up the first waterfall, fell into the cold water and panicked. I was already in the water and was able to swim to her and bring her to the side. Her confidence was knocked though and she did not want to continue. That was fine and she and I walked up the road at the side of the falls and met the party at the top.

Challenge certainly was an appropriate name for these outdoor activities, although on the last day we always did a far less demanding walk out of Beddgelert, before calling in at Lucy's Café for a drink and scones with jam and cream. Wonderful memories.

Ski Trips to the Alps

Students at Alsager, for many years, have been fortunate to have had the opportunity to take part in ski trips to the French, Austrian, Swiss and Italian Alps. For many of those years, this opportunity passed me by, for although I had numerous invitations to accompany the school parties, as a non-skier, I had always turned them down. I was soon to learn that this had been a big mistake. In February 1995 Steve Marshal, the team leader and others in the team - Pat Sutton, Brenda Steel (Thomas), Stella Spratley, Graham Shaw, Peter Lloyd, Mike Holland, Dan Margolan and Jason Howells - finally persuaded me to join them in the small French resort of Risoul.

Ski group in the snow outside our hotel.

After a few days of lessons with our student skiers, returning from the slopes exhausted and covered in bruises, I began to get the hang of this skiing and never looked back. I continued to go on student, staff and family ski trips and skiing has become a central

Ski Leader Steve Marshall and my ski coach Pat Sutton.

part of my life to this day. I have to pay a particular tribute to Pat Sutton, a really stylish and fearless skier, as most of the improvement I made in subsequent years was due to tucking in behind Pat and following her tracks down the mountain.

School ski trips were great fun and it was always a fantastic experience to be with the students and staff both on 'the white stuff' and socially. It is a shame that ski trips are expensive and not everyone's 'cup of tea', as the experience you get standing on top of a 3000 metre peak, looking out across the Alps, is second to none. Equally, the feeling that comes over your body, when you are just about to ski off that peak, can either be one of invigoration or intimidation, or most likely a mixture of both. Great fun!

Having been led on ski trips for many years by Mr Marshall and Ms Sutton, on February 2002, it fell to me to lead a trip to Valmeinier/ Valloire in the Maurienne Valley. In the March 2002 Headline, I wrote the following account of the trip:

"Apart from a few stressful hours on arrival, when we were unable to get into our apartments, the trip went very smoothly and there were few cross words all round. This year we experienced 'doorstep skiing' straight out of the apartments on to the slopes. In all my previous years we have had to bus to the slopes and I have to say I did not miss the loading of skis and boots on and off the coach one bit! Another first was the use of 'walkie-talkies' to improve communication between staff in different parts of the resort and so enhance safety and security. We did, however, get many a strange

glance from our fellow skiers as 'Welsh Dragon' tried to make contact with 'Bionic Man', 'Supermum' and 'Blondie' while going up a chair lift.

The students were a pleasure to be with. Not only was their behaviour exemplary, on almost all occasions, but also they made excellent progress with their skiing. The instructors were most complimentary about their attitude, courage and willingness to listen".

One of the early ski trips led by Joyce and Jeff Halsall and Dave Throp. Great jumper on Mr Halsall, C&A's best! 1988.

Ski trips continue to this day. Graham Shaw took over from me as leader and then Joyce and Jeff Halsall, who used to run the very early trips back in the eighties, took the leader's role again. During the most recent period Marc Bennett has been the ski supremo, ably supported by Holly Salt, Alex Taylor and Emma Dougherty. Long may the trips continue!

Local Studies

Before the advent of the 1988 Education Reform Act and the introduction of the National Curriculum, things were a little more 'relaxed', in that not all students had to follow courses that led to external 'O' Level and CSE Qualifications. One of the non-exam courses that Alsager offered at the time was Local Studies. This was broadly a practical history and geography course that focused on the local area and made extensive use of the school minibus. As I was Head of Humanities back in the mid-Eighties, I taught the course. Usually, it was restricted to about 12 students, so the minibus could be used, and it mainly attracted boys. My aim was to try to get the lads out of the classroom and involved in practical studies, as much as possible.

We covered lots of activities and went to lots of local places of interest. This one particular Friday afternoon, I thought I would take them onto the 'Bosley Cloud' above Congleton. It was a lovely, sunny, crisp, winter's afternoon and there was a covering of snow on the Cloud. The Plan - practice their map reading skills, watch the planes coming and going at Manchester Airport through our binoculars and have a game of snowballs. Having parked the bus at the back of the Cloud, we ascended easily, spent some time plane watching and even the snowballing was quite civilised. Things were going well. I got out the maps and showed the lads their route down the front side of the Cloud, towards Congleton and the rendezvous point where we would meet. Nine lads would follow this route and one of the group would come back with me as he was a little 'vulnerable'.

I drove the minibus to the meeting point and anticipated a 30 minute wait. An hour later, there was still no sign of the group. By this time the weather was changing and snow was coming in from the west. Getting a little anxious, I got out the binoculars and scanned the Cloud. There was no sign of my group which was a relief to know they were not still up on the hill. Conveniently, there was a man sledging on a slope with his two young children and very kindly he agreed to drive around the Cloud to see if they had taken another path and come onto the road at a different place. Fifteen minutes later, the man had returned but there was still no sign of the boys. Anxiety levels rising, he invited me into his house and allowed me to phone school. With great embarrassment, I had to tell Jim Andrews that I had lost my class on the Cloud. Fortunately, he was very reassuring.

Thankfully, I knew that nobody in their right senses would accost this group of lads. They were very 'streetwise' and could handle

144

themselves, if not a map. About an hour and half after the arranged meeting time, a police panda car (an Astra) headed towards me, with 8 lads strewn in various positions inside. Never had I been so relieved. They had misread the map, come out on a different road, gone to the first house to ask the way but the lady closed the door on them. They then decided to head down into Congleton, found the police station and got a lift back. What could I say? I thanked the policeman and the man who drove round the Cloud and said well done to my lads for showing common sense, if 'dodgy' map reading skills.

I got back to Alsager School about 5.30 pm, having dropped off the boys at home. Jim Andrews was waiting for me! *"You need a stiff drink m'boy"*. He took me home for a couple of single malts. That was the sort of Head, Jim Andrews was.

At the end of two years, I had become quite close to this group of boys, particularly, having spent so much time with them outside the classroom. Just before they were due to leave school, I asked them what they would like to do, one last time, as a treat before leaving. They thought about this and decided they would like to hire a narrow boat and go for a trip along one of the canals. A little surprised but not daunted, I eventually found a small narrow boat at a marina near to Northwich.

On the day, we headed north along the Trent-Mersey canal towards Runcorn. Things were going well, we had moored up for a snack before we came to a fairly low tunnel. Before entering, I explained to the group how in the days of horse-pulled boats, the bargees used to 'leg it' through the tunnels while the horses went over the top. The lads were quite taken by this idea and wanted to have a go. As it was a small barge, stupidly I agreed. I switched off the engine, the boys got on the roof and tried to leg it with their feet on the walls. At the far end of the tunnel, to my dismay, the boat was covered with 'gunge' pulled off the walls and ceiling by the boy's feet. It was a real mess! Still, we had some mops on board, so it was 'swab the decks me hearties'. The cleaning seemed under control until someone shouted *"Jeffrey's overboard sir"*. I looked around and there he was desperately hanging on with one hand, trying to keep his head above water. The strange thing was nobody moved at first as everyone was too busy laughing. I must admit it was funny but eventually we did pull him back on board, none the worse for his dip in the canal. Fortunately, Craig another member of our group and a keen Scout, had brought a change of clothes which he kindly lent to Jeffrey.

We all got back safely after another memorable adventure beyond the four walls of the classroom. I probably broke a thousand and one risk assessment regulations by today's standards but those students had fun on the day and experiences which they probably will never forget. In today's climate of strict health and safety regulations and closely scrutinised risk assessment policies, it is doubtful whether some of the adventures outlined above would be allowed to take place. I am also certain that most teachers, for very obvious and understandable reasons, would be reluctant to put their careers on the line in the same way. As Chair of Governors I would have to say that this is a good thing. Safety of students is paramount, but somewhere deep inside me, I can't help feeling that we have lost that sense of adventure which we once had, a sense that was instilled in me, all those years ago, growing up in the coal mining valleys of South Wales.

Staff Cricket

During the Eighties and Nineties, Thursday evenings in Summer meant one thing–staff cricket matches. They really were a highlight of the week. A twenty over match followed by a convivial gathering, at a local hostelry, to talk about the finer points of our game or where we went wrong. There were a number of fierce local rivalries, most notably against Sandbach School and Crewe and Alsager College. I used to keep wicket and against these teams I stood about 10 metres behind the stumps, as Alvan Ikoku and Mike Holland, our star bowlers, rained the balls down at ferocious pace, for me to take at shoulder height. Bowling was our real strength, as we had Steve Marshall, Graham Lee and Graham Marsden, from the Art Department, who could also take the wickets.

For me the real concern was when Head of Music, John Turner came on to bowl. Being a slow, sorry very slow, bowler he used to toss the ball so far in the air that by the time it bounced, the batsman had so much time to turn and smash the ball straight at me. I used to have nightmares about John's bowling on a Wednesday night.

Most of the team were male but occasionally Val Hollins and Hilda Clarke would play for us. Both Val and Hilda could really 'turn their arm' and it was no surprise to us if they came away with a fist full of wickets, but to the opposition it certainly was a shock! Mr Andrews always used to umpire but few could ever remember him raising his finger to give a person out, on an LBW call.

Staff Cricket Team circa 1988.

It was at a match against The College, for which he was a little late, that Mr Andrews broke the news quietly in my ear, that the Governors had just appointed me Deputy Head. Personally for me, a most memorable evening, particularly as I also caught out behind the wickets, Paul Holmes, their British Colleges opening bat. Other

Parents Cricket team circa 1990.

enjoyable annual staff cricket fixtures were against the New Inn pub on the Sandbach Road, the Parents and the Sixth Form.

A one off charity staff game which always stays in my mind, took place one lunch time, again way back in the mid-eighties. Probably inadvisable today but after a serious 'man to man' with Jim Andrews, I eventually persuaded him to agree to a Staff v Students Rugby Match. The students, mainly from Mr Marshall's and my rugby team in Year 11, with a few imports from the Sixth Form, against whatever motley crew, he and I could muster together from the staff. It certainly wasn't a case of us doing a 'Boris Johnson', battering little boys.

We may have been heavier but most of them were as big and certainly faster. In the end the staff managed to get twelve players together, the students had double that number wanting to make their mark on the game. We decided on 5-man scrums, health and safety prevailing, not to mention the shortage of numbers on our part. Staff team members on the day included: Peter Lloyd, Dave

Rowley, Hedley Austen, Alvan Ikoku, Steve Marshall, John Lyne, Derek Brooks, Wyn Jones, Dave Throp, Tim Upfield, Carl Gaskell, Graham Marsden. Although the actual score must remain in the 'depths of time', I do believe the staff were victorious by a narrow margin, in front of a large crowd of students and staff. The game was played in excellent spirit and thankfully there were no serious injuries, though plenty of aching bones and stiff limbs during afternoon school and on subsequent days. Great fun was had by all.

Another somewhat less harmonious Staff versus Sixth Form football game took place shortly after I arrived at the school in 1978. The Reverend John Hughes, who was Head of Sixth Form, officiated, very smartly clad in his FA Referee's uniform. Immediately the game started you could tell there would be 'no quarter asked or given'. Fouls started going in and the game became very physical, with culprits on both sides. John did his very best to keep control but eventually he had to resort to sending off a Sixth Form Student and Mr Tony Cunningham, a fiery Cumbrian teacher of History and Politics. The mood did not improve and half way through the second half, the Reverend Hughes abandoned the game. A great shame but the correct decision on the afternoon.

The interesting thing about Tony Cunningham was that he left the school a year or two later, to do Voluntary Service Overseas. He returned to become Mayor of Workington, before going on to become Labour MP for Workington and a Junior Agriculture Minister in Tony Blair's Government. I last saw him a number of years ago at a funeral in Workington, where we reminisced over a few beers afterwards and he invited me on the behind the scenes tour of the Palace of Westminster.

As I remember, staff football was resurrected again towards the end of the Eighties, with the arrival of a number of staff keen on the sport, including Technology teacher Andy Pennance. He wrote:

"Games were arranged on a Friday evening after school against other local school staff teams, including Holmes Chapel

Comprehensive, Sandbach Boys, Fallibroome High, Victoria High and Heathfield High. We tried to organise most of our fixtures at home on the new astro turf. Five-a-side matches were also a feature in the sports hall. Results were mixed, as was the fitness and skill level of the staff team and we were not averse to bringing in the occasional 'ringer' to boost the chance of a victory. Nevertheless the spirit was willing, as was the enthusiasm. Mr Alvan Ikoku was usually the referee and depending on availability, the following staff were keen to play: Graham Marsden, Graham Lee, John Lyne, Tony Clare, Mel Smith, Mike Holland, Steve Marshall, Ernie Charlton, Trevor Sparrow, Danny Margolan, Terry Sharrock, Lindsay Purcell, Andy Pennance, John Lee, Nick Churchill and Steve Smith".

Chapter 10: The Middlebrook Years

Richard Middlebrook took over as Headteacher in September 2011. He wrote in the Head's Log.

"David Black retired as Headteacher of Alsager School after 18 wonderful years of service. The school has gone from strength to strength, under his leadership. On a personal note, David was very warm and welcoming, in terms of handover to me. He handled his retirement and my succession with great professionalism".

It was an incredibly smooth transfer between Heads.

Richard Middlebrook on taking up his new Headship at Alsager School.

So what did we know about the Sixth Head of Alsager School, Richard Middlebrook? He trained as a teacher of RE, with secondary PE. He had previously taught for 20 years in Oldham, St Helens, Wigan and most recently Trafford, where he was a Deputy Head. Sport is his great passion. He played rugby for Preston Grasshoppers, inexplicably supports Sunderland FC and has a growing love of skiing with his family. I am reliably informed that the students who were involved in his interview process, were well impressed that he could explain clearly, the football 'offside' law, which was one of their questions. It is my belief, that he can also explain the rugby 'offside' law which probably makes him a sporting legend.

September 2011 also saw the appointment of the school's first ever Student Voice Co-ordinator, Dan Hancock. Dan had just finished his 'A' Levels at school and was appointed to this role in his gap year, to gain valuable experience before studying for a teaching qualification to become a primary teacher. As Student Voice Co-ordinator, Dan's role included organising year council groups across the school and liaising with the Student Leadership Team on various projects, to raise the profile of 'Student Voice' within the school.

He also spent a day or two per week in our partner primary schools, again working with their school councils, leading projects and various assemblies and supporting some sports activities. All in all, Dan had a great year and the role was so successful, other appointments were made in subsequent years. They were:

2012-13 - Kieran Puez

2013-14 - Victoria Hibberd

2014-15 - Emily Clarke

2015-16 - Imogen Gregory

Sadly, budget constraints prevented the role from continuing beyond 2016.

On 1st September 2013, Alsager School became an Academy. (Actually it became Alsager Multi Academy Trust, AMAT but more on this later). This was the most significant change to the school's status since it became a comprehensive school in 1971. Academies are publicly funded schools which operate outside local authority control. The Government described them as 'independent state-funded schools'.

Essentially, Alsager School now had greater freedom over its finances, its curriculum and teachers' pay and conditions, should it wish to depart from national agreements. As well as receiving funds directly from the Government, it also received money which would have been held back by Cheshire East, to provide extra services across all schools, such as Special Educational Needs. When Alsager School converted to academy status, this 'top slice' was in the region of £250,000.

Although this surge in the growth of academies dates back to the Cameron Coalition Government's Academies Act of 2010, the actual idea was the brainchild of Prime Minister Tony Blair and his education adviser, Andrew Adonis. Academies were introduced through the Learning and Skills Act 2000, to boost struggling schools in deprived inner-city areas. Since then the number of academies has grown to almost 8,000. Most secondary schools now have academy status, as do almost a third of primary schools.

Academies fall into two main groups: Converter Academies and Sponsor Academies. Alsager School is a Converter Academy, as it was deemed successful enough to 'convert' to academy status, in order to benefit from increased autonomy.

Sponsor Academies have sponsors such as businesses, faith communities, universities, voluntary groups or other schools. These tend to be schools deemed to be underperforming by OFSTED and have become academies to improve their performance, with the support of their sponsor. For instance, Alsager Highfields Primary School changed its status in September 2020 from a 'Community School' to a 'Sponsor Academy', with Alsager School being its sponsor.

Alsager School is in fact a Multi Academy Trust, AMAT, rather than a Single Academy Trust. A MAT is a group or 'chain' of schools who work in partnership with each other, for the benefit of all. When the school converted to academy status in 2013, it sensibly opted to become a MAT, so that ultimately other schools could join the partnership.

There were obvious advantages to working as a group of schools - creating common policies, streamlining school organisation and systems, sharing expertise, exchanging staff. The School decided that the MAT would remain quite small and that all schools in the partnership would be fairly local. This is in contrast to many MATs around the country, which have 30-40 schools, dispersed over a wide geographical area.

AMAT is a 'not for profit company'. All the school staff are employed by the Trust and a Board of Trustees is responsible for the performance of the academies in the Trust. Having said this, it is the individual School Governing Bodies who are responsible for overseeing the day to day educational and financial performance of the school, its leaders, staff and students. Only in exceptional circumstances, for example serious educational or financial under-performance, would AMAT Trustees, take a more 'hands on' approach.

Weston Primary School chose to join AMAT at Easter 2018 and Alsager Highfields Primary School became part of the partnership in September 2020. In anticipation of additional schools joining AMAT, Richard Middlebrook was appointed Executive Headteacher of the MAT in September 2018 and his senior Deputy Head, Mrs Andrea O'Neill, became Head of School in September 2019. Having oversight of all three schools meant that more of Richard Middlebrook's time was being spent in the two primary schools. As a result, Mrs O'Neill became more central to the overall leadership and management of Alsager School.

The 'academy badge' isn't necessarily associated with success. In 2017, research by the Education Policy Institute found that turning schools into academies didn't automatically drive up standards, with some of the lowest performing primary and secondary schools in England being academies. Indeed, the research was also critical of the DfE's inability to prevent a *"succession of high-profile academy failures"*, which have been costly to the tax payer and damaging to children's education.

The discerning reader will be aware, of course, that whatever the status of a school, the really important keys to success are the quality of leadership and staff and the relationship developed between leadership, staff, students and parents (all partners in the education of a young person). Fortunately, the ingredients for success are, and have been, in abundance at Alsager School since the inception of 'education for all' way back in 1971.

Alsager School, however, certainly did achieve almost immediate success and recognition from its newly gained academy status, for in July 2015, the DfE approved the school as an 'Academy Sponsor'. This meant that it was now in a position to support schools, which were under-performing for whatever reason.

This accolade was quickly followed by the outstanding OFSTED judgement in February 2016 and again in July 2016, the DfE designated the school a 'National Support School' and Headteacher, Richard Middlebrook, a National Leader of Education.

Recognition did not stop there. In July, Mr Middlebrook learned he was in a shortlist of four, for Secondary Headteacher of the Year at the 2016 Pearson Education, National Teaching Awards Ceremony in London. Although, he did not win the 'gold award', he was presented with the 'silver award', for his outstanding achievements at Alsager School.

Richard Middlebrook receiving his Secondary Headteacher of the Year Award 2016.

We were all incredibly proud of our Headteacher, for as leader, Mr Middlebrook reflected the overall performance of everyone at the School.

In 2017 and 2018 Alsager was shortlisted for the Cheshire School of the Year and in both these years it was the most oversubscribed school in Cheshire, Staffordshire and Stoke-on-Trent.

These were all impressive achievements in such a short time span (2013-18), for everyone connected to the school. Looking back, there may be some 'historic parallels' to be drawn here, with the rapid successes and gains in reputation which the newly created Comprehensive School achieved under Jim Andrews and his staff, throughout the 1970s. To go from a relatively small secondary modern to large comprehensive, in which impressive numbers of students were gaining places in Britain's top universities and on the most prestigious apprenticeships, was no mean feat and something incredibly tangible for Alsager, as a community, to celebrate.

In September 2017, another small yet very significant celebration took place in the staff room at school, organised by personnel manager Annette Owen. It was to celebrate 35 years of direct employment by the school of a super lady called Mavis Broad. Mavis is one of the school community's unsung heroes, who enters and leaves school quietly and largely unnoticed, but remains a key member of our team. She is our Food/Textile Technician and cleaner. What was so significant about Mavis' length of service was that prior to being employed directly by the school, Mavis was employed by Cheshire County Council but deployed at the school. In all, this took Mavis' working life at Alsager School close to 50 years. There is some uncertainty about the exact number of years as records do not go back that far. What an incredible achievement and demonstration of loyalty. A milestone worthy of inclusion in any history of Alsager School.

In September 2019, Alsager School was the designated lead school for the Cheshire and Wirral Maths Hub. The Maths teacher leading this initiative is Jane Watts. This is one of 40 Maths Hubs nationally, whose role it is to improve the quality of Maths teaching. Maths Hubs provide high quality professional development for maths teachers, much of which is based on the 'mastery' approach which has proved so successful in Asia. Maths hubs provide programmes for teachers from Early Years right through to 'A' Level.

In spite of the increasing central influence over the curriculum which I have alluded to on several occasions throughout this story, it is heart-warming to know that in 2020, constant, curriculum debate is still alive and well at Alsager School, led by Deputy Head, Liane Young. It is thoughtful, thorough, transparent and driven by a consideration of what best meets the needs of our young people, not by the need to please the latest OFSTED framework.

I want to focus here on two main strands under discussion:

- The move towards a more 'comprehensive' approach to post-16 education. Something, you will have learned, which has been debated on a number of occasions in the past.
- The structure of the KS3/KS4 Curriculum. In other words, should the school change back to a more conventional three year KS3.

The move towards a broader sixth form provision was in part based on a moral decision and in part a financial one. As a comprehensive secondary school we were still offering post-16 pathways to fewer than 60% of our young people. The remainder were travelling outside Alsager to continue their education. The popularity of the school was growing and greater numbers of students wanted to stay beyond the age of sixteen. The school also needed to get back to a state of affairs where the Sixth Form covered its own costs, through larger student numbers and average group sizes.

For some students a move to one of the local colleges was absolutely the right decision and there were many courses we simply could not run as effectively as the colleges. However, there were a variety of less costly, vocational and technical courses which required little specialist equipment and accommodation. These courses had grown in reputation and the school believed parents would now be willing to accept them as a 'bone fide' part of the post-16 curriculum,

Among the first subjects to be introduced at the school were Business Studies, Public Services and Travel and Tourism. The offer in 2020 included Criminology, Sports Studies, Applied Science, Media Studies and Health and Social Care. The challenge for the school was that the DFE regularly kept changing which courses and qualifications secured funding and performance points, so courses had to change. An example was Public Services, which offered some exciting pathways into Higher Education and employment. Unfortunately the funding was withdrawn, so the school could no longer offer it.

It is worth noting that a Traineeship pathway was also introduced in 2014 by the then Deputy Head, Sonia Cross and the Sixth Form Team. It met a need for some students who had been successful and happy at the school but were not ready to enter the world of work. This pathway offered support for these students, building up time on work placement and coupling this with qualifications in work skills, Maths and English GCSE.

The KS3/4 issue developed into a really thought provoking debate. Nationally there was a great deal of external pressure to return to a more conventional three year KS3, two year KS4 structure.

Initially, Alsager had moved to a three year KS4 in 2008 for very good reasons, the main one being to take pressure off students in their GCSE years. More time was given to students to complete their syllabuses and they were offered an alternative 'enrichment' programme, which would remove them from the 'treadmill' of examinations. PINC was born at this time and was to become a feature of school life. The central premise of the curriculum re-structure was certainly not about improving GCSE results but more about the well-being of the students.

By 2019, Amanda Spielman, Head of OFSTED, made it clear that schools with only a two year KS3 programme would have to make a very strong defence of its rationale for choosing such a structure. However, the central focus for the curriculum debate at Alsager was 'what was best for the school and its young people', not 'what OFSTED wanted to see'. Unquestionably, the shorter KS3 had significant benefits for KS4 as highlighted above.

However, when reviewing the existing arrangement, there were some uncomfortable truths. Most students were dropping foreign languages at the age of 12/13 years. Some had only been taught by a subject specialist for 18 months at this stage. Similarly in Humanities, whilst most students opted for a single subject, they were dropping Geography or History, after very little overall study time. This would not happen in the 'Independent' sector. Why?

Because these subjects open many doors. The data and feedback from employers told us that these were valuable subjects, yet the school was allowing large numbers of students to stop studying them, at a very early stage.

Our school leaders needed to acknowledge that they appreciated the value of these subjects and therefore should make sure that students had greater experience of them. These subjects were also perceived by many students as being 'hard' at KS3, which affected the uptake at KS4. Giving extra time to experience and understand them and using specialists to teach them, would hopefully develop more of a love of the subjects. New arrangements have now been put in place, so that all students will continue with a foreign language, History and Geography into Year 9 but there will still be two elements of choice, in a clever curriculum arrangement.

A central pillar of this curriculum re-design and development is SPIRIT - Self-Regulation; Participation; Integrity; Resilient; Inspired; Tolerant. The SPIRIT ethos is at the heart of everything the school does and is focused around a main set of values. These values are incorporated into the school's Behaviour for Learning programme, they are embedded into all subject curricula, including SPIRIT learning, formerly the PHSE curriculum. They are the focus of assemblies and underpin all pastoral work. The hope is that a focus on these values and an emphasis on a common language and approach, will enhance relationships between staff and students and further develop student character.

The PINC week of activities was also re-named SPIRIT in keeping with the above changes. From everything you have read, you will know that the school has always prided itself on the opportunities offered to students to support their academic studies. It has always aimed to give ALL pupils a broad and wide experience of school life. The purpose of SPIRIT Enrichment is to enable students to engage with skills, ideas and activities which they can see have an immediate link with the world outside school, as well as in.

There was no SPIRIT week in 2020 because of the Covid Lockdown of schools but in 2019, students had unique and exciting opportunities to demonstrate the SPIRIT values through many different activities designed to develop new skills.

New Spirit Logo was designed during the Coronavirus lockdown period by Camille Dovey,

A multitude of activities were on offer within school and the local area. For example, Rugby Union with a Crewe & Nantwich RUFC coach, Archery with the Alsager Scout Group, an in-house Rock School, a Cake Pops kitchen and a Hat Design for the 'Mad Hatters' Tea Party. There was a Photography Exhibition based on the landscape and wildlife of Alsager, while some worked with local makeup artist, Jody, on a Make Up and Special Effects Masterclass or created bespoke jewellery with Alsager's Beading Amazing team. Further afield, students visited the Catalyst Science Discovery Centre in Widnes, went Ice Skating and Skiing, visited the Lego Innovation Studio, navigated the Peak District, captured the flag whilst orienteering at Brereton, visited the Blue John Cavern in Castleton, played golf and designed a clay mask at the Gladstone Pottery Museum. Alongside these day trips, a group of students went on a London Theatre visit, to see School of Rock and Phantom of the Opera. Finally some went on a visit to Krakow in Poland, which included a moving trip to Auschwitz.

Chapter 11: The Governing Body

In the nineties and throughout the new millennium, the role of the Governing Body took on a much greater significance and there were distinct structural changes. The main changes were far less political representation and greater parental and staff involvement. Additionally, the local community, in the broadest sense, was given the opportunity to be co-opted. Schools were encouraged to consider the range of skills and experience which their governors could bring to support the development of the school. Since the erosion of Local Authority powers, the Governors became the key people to hold the school and its management to account. Accordingly, their responsibilities were far more significant than previously and Governors needed to appreciate the demands that were being placed upon them, in terms of time commitment and role fulfilment.

In essence, a Governing Body has three core functions;

1. To ensure clarity of vision, ethos and strategic direction.

2. To hold leaders to account for the educational performance of the school and its students and the performance management of its staff.

3. To oversee the financial performance of the school and make sure its money is well spent.

In all the years I have been involved with the Governing Body of Alsager School, as Deputy Head, Governor and now Chair of Governors, I have always been impressed with the dedicated and professional way in which the group has operated as a team. The manner in which all three Heads, Leadership Teams and Governors have engaged with each other, has been transparent, harmonious, yet challenging. The school could not have been in safer, more responsible hands. Another feature of the Governing Body down the years, was the close personal tie that individual governors had with the school. There were many occasions when every governor was a parent or had been a parent, which inevitably brought a real commitment to the school.

During that early period of enormous change, from 1955 through those years of secondary modern schooling, to the era of firmly establishing comprehensive education in Alsager, there was one constant. Alderman John Hollinshead, OBE. was Chair of Governors. A remarkable man and a great servant of the school. He retired on December 11th 1985, having served 30 years as Chairman, a feat that will never be repeated. He was presented with a silver salver and glass decanter, in recognition of his outstanding achievements, on February 26th 1986.

Chair of Governors, Alderman John Hollinshead and Jim Andrews toasting George Bull, Head of Design and Technology on his retirement.

John Hollinshead was succeeded by Cllr. Jeremy Smith as Chair, who held this position until 18th June 1986, when Co. Cllr. Derek Bould succeeded him. Cllr Bould, expertly continued in the Chair for seven years. His wisdom and knowledge of County Council and Borough affairs was 'second to none', which always proved invaluable to school decision making. In January 1993, Co. Cllr Shirley Jones took over from Derek, who remained on the Governing Body as Vice Chair. Anyone who has met Shirley will know her to be a 'force of nature' and she carried out the role with her usual energy and determination. She was Chair of the Education Committee at County Hall, which also brought its benefits at times. Cllr. Bould returned for another period as Chair, replacing Cllr Jones, before Mr Ian White took over on Cllr Bould's retirement, in September 2001.

Although, as I have indicated, all the previous Chairs performed their duties with great professionalism and distinction, Ian took the role a stage further. He was very much 'hands on' and visible in the school. He would pop in on a more regular basis, visit departments, go on school trips, sometimes abroad, and always deliver a humorous speech at Christmas and the end of the Summer Term. All of this was much appreciated by the staff, who found it easy to engage with him.

At the end of 2011, Ian retired as Chair of Governors after ten years. Mr Allan Ward replaced him as Chair, having been Vice Chair for a good many years. Allan lived but a 'stone's throw' from school, so was always there when the school needed him. He was shrewd and thoughtful in all matters relating to school governance but his real strength was in overseeing the financial performance. He guided the school through some difficult years, in terms of budgetary planning.

Allan Ward stepped down as Chair of the Alsager School Governing Body on May 17th 2017, to concentrate on his role as Chair of AMAT Trustees and I replaced him as the seventh Chair of Governors in Alsager School's history, since 1955. Only time will tell, how I measure up alongside my illustrious predecessors?

Chapter 12: Sad Times

Generally, the overwhelming feelings throughout my time at Alsager School were of happiness and fulfilment, but there were times of great sadness. These related mainly to the untimely deaths of some students and staff during the years I taught at the school. It is heart-wrenching when members of the school community, with so much youth, talent, energy and enthusiasm, are taken from us so early in their lives, whether during their time at school or in the years shortly afterwards.

Year 7 Geography lessons used to include a Geology unit in the graveyard of Christ Church. The church was always very accommodating and the children very respectful of the location. While the classes were at work, I used to take time to stroll round the newer part of the cemetery and pay my respects to former students and staff who either had headstones or commemorative plaques there. I found it a very moving experience.

My personal reflections about Alsager School would be incomplete without mentioning a few friends and colleagues, who had a huge impact on teaching and learning while they were at the school.

Jill Bristow (Riley) started as a young English teacher, in her first post, on the same day as me in September 1978. Not an easy role to fulfil at Alsager, as her mother Sheila Riley was Deputy Head. This did not bother Jill! In typical fashion she got on with the job and quickly made her mark, becoming a gifted teacher. Jill stayed at the school all her working life and when I retired in July 2007, she took over my role as Deputy Head. Sadly, at the height of her career Jill became ill and after a brave fight had to give in to MND. She was greatly missed by everyone at school and by me.

The second person was Mel Smith. Mel was a terrific Maths teacher, first and foremost. He was a very logical person, as you would expect being a mathematician, with huge amounts of common sense. Mel became a well-respected Head of Year, before being promoted to Senior Teacher in charge of all the data management in the school and then Assistant Head. Mel and I spent a great deal of time together in a tiny room completing the school timetable, at which he was expert. We also shared a lot of our inner-most thoughts and many amusing stories, during those long hours spent together. He retired early to spend more time with his wife and family but sadly died shortly after his retirement. I was honoured to be asked to give his eulogy.

Keith Plant was another member of staff who dedicated his life to Alsager School. He began his career there in 1976 as a young English and Drama teacher and rose through the ranks to become Head of Drama, Director of Sixth Form, Assistant Head and Deputy Head with Jill Bristow. He was hugely talented in so many different ways, both in and out of the classroom. An inspiring teacher, director of school and community productions, talented writer, photographer and cricketer. A person with a shrewd knowledge of racehorses and worth talking to before placing a bet! Keith retired in July 2010 after 34 years of loyal service but sadly died, still in his prime, in 2020 after a short illness.

Mike Elkin did live a long and active life after his retirement but I could not write this epic without commenting on his contribution to school life, as a Geography and Maths teacher and especially as a much loved Senior Tutor. Mike was a genuinely kind, affable person and these attributes transferred to those around him. Mike seldom had to raise his voice, as the students and staff he taught and worked with, wanted to please him and do his bidding. This is a rare quality to have in the teaching profession and life in general. Mike was also a man of our community, doing remarkable work to help others.

Finally, of course, there was Jim Andrews himself. Jim died aged 81 years in 2013. The very eloquent Keith Plant wrote the following piece, which was published in the national Guardian Newspaper's 'Other Lives' column, shortly after Jim's death. A fitting obituary, as

Jim was an avid reader of that newspaper.

"Jim Andrews was the first headteacher of Alsager Comprehensive School. He inherited a modestly achieving secondary modern school, as it turned comprehensive, in a fairly prosperous Cheshire dormitory town.

On his arrival in 1970, he saw his first task as persuading parents who had previously sent their offspring to grammar and independent schools, in neighbouring towns, that their children's education would be safe in his hands. How right they were to trust him: 'O' Level results were immediately excellent and many of the first cohort went to Oxbridge Colleges.

Consequently, his impact on the town far exceeded education. Housing estates grew as people moved in to work at expanding ICT, Higher Education and other organisations, safe in the knowledge that their children were guaranteed a first class education, irrespective of ability. Many of his staff felt that local estate agents should have offered him a retainer - but he would certainly have refused. Meanwhile the school grew to 1,700 students in a town of only 15,000 inhabitants.

Jim was born in Bolton during the depression and was a lifelong fan of Bolton Wanderers and Lancashire Cricket Club. He never forgot the poverty of his childhood (his parents could not afford to buy him football boots) and was a lifelong socialist. He began reading the Guardian as a child and he continued to be passionate about its liberal values. His grammar school education enabled him to escape the poverty trap and he was determined to give the same opportunity to the thousands of children who found themselves under his wing.

He was a devoted husband and father and immensely proud of the achievements of his daughters Alison and Fiona, both of whom attended his school. He loved the outdoors: sailing, climbing and walking were deep passions, often followed by a pint and a malt whisky.

Under his stewardship, Alsager Comprehensive's staff room became 'a great hunting ground' for other schools and many of his colleagues found themselves promoted to senior positions elsewhere. No child dared question his manifest authority, yet he was compassionate, wise and a great listener. 'Respect' was written through him like a stick of Bolton rock!"

Jim Andrews doing one of the activities he loved best - sailing round the Hebrides.

Chapter 13: A Year like no other!

And so to the Academic Year of 2019-20. It started so wonderfully well. Mr Middlebrook wrote in his opening blog of the year:

"Welcome back... I hope everyone had an enjoyable and relaxing summer break and feels refreshed and ready to face the challenges of a new school year".

Little did he know what lay ahead!

"The highlight of any summer holiday is always the external exam results and the two cohorts of 2019 did fantastically well. I am delighted that for so many of our young people, all the hard work they put in preparing for those challenging exams paid off and they achieved the results they deserved. Congratulations to them all. The school once again performed incredibly well, based on every key performance indicator, compared to local and national data. Alsager is once again riding high!"

At the start of the year the school was informed that it had been awarded the prestigious AcSeed Accreditation, for the excellent work achieved in creating a supportive culture of kindness and for the staff's success in fostering strategies for wellbeing and resilience amongst students.

Later in the month, we were to learn that the school featured highly in the Sunday Times list of Good Schools.

A very strong Sixth Form Student Leadership Team had been appointed when still in Year 12, with Shay Norman as Head Boy and Simone Spibey as Head Girl. This team organised a very successful Charity Coffee Morning midway through the Autumn Term, followed by a Fancy Dress Sponsored Walk, which saw members of Queen, the cast of Grease, Donald Trump and the team of Ghostbusters, set off from the school for a five mile walk. It was a very successful end to a great year of fundraising by the 6th form, with over £2000 being raised for Visyon and Headway.

On 24th September, the annual Awards and Pastoral Celebration Evening provided an opportunity to celebrate the academic and pastoral achievements of Year 7 to 11 students for the year 2018-19. College Awards were given to recognise the school's SPIRIT values which are key qualities encouraged in all students. Mrs O'Neill, Head of School, spoke about the importance of such celebrations in helping to embed aspiration and develop a culture of learning, kindness and respect.

The evening also provided an opportunity to celebrate individual successes amongst Sixth Form students for that year. Awards included the 'Katy Wright Science Bursary' which was kindly donated by Anne and John Wright in memory of their daughter Katy, a former student and subsequent teacher, who sadly died from a rare form of cancer at the age of 30 years. Each year Katy's parents wanted to recognise the achievement of an outstanding female scientist from the Sixth Form, in the hope it would inspire young female students to pursue a career in Science. This year, the award was presented to Zoe Reed, now studying Medicine at Oxford University. Other Sixth Form award winners that evening were Daisy Sawdon, Tiffany Powell and Jakob Harper.

In October 'A' Level Politics students welcomed Fiona Bruce, MP for Congleton, to 'Question Time' at Alsager School. The students applied their knowledge of UK Politics to present Mrs Bruce with a series of challenging and thought-provoking questions on a range of issues, from Boris Johnson's leadership to Brexit and the environment. The students thoroughly enjoyed this opportunity for an 'up close' discussion with a Westminster politician and felt their political opinions were valued and respected. Mrs Bruce commended the Alsager students who took part in the successful event, commenting:

"I thoroughly enjoyed meeting the students. Their questions were

interesting and thought provoking without being aggressive in any way, for which I thank and commend them. The event should be held as an example to many of my professional colleagues, on how political discourse should be conducted. The students I met were a credit to the school and it would be a pleasure to welcome any of them to Parliament".

The official opening of the new Sixth Form Centre and Dining Hall took place on November 7th 2019. The Sixth Form Building not only included five new classrooms on the upper floor but also a marvellous independent study area, café area and office space on the ground floor. The dining hall is now a much more spacious and attractive environment, in which the students can enjoy their breaks and lunch times. In addition to this, the school has also gained 2 science labs and 6 new classrooms in the Parker Building. Mr Middlebrook in praise of the completed project commented:

"We are absolutely delighted with our finished school expansion. All this work has improved our site enormously, giving us the additional space we need to accommodate the increasing number of students and created a fantastic learning environment for our young people and staff. I would especially like to thank Cheshire East local authority for funding this expansion and for all their support throughout the project. The fundamental role of any school is to serve its local community, and Cheshire East's investment has made this possible for the young people of Alsager.

Finally, I would like to thank all the staff involved in managing this project, especially our site, finance and catering teams. It has involved a huge amount of work over the last 18 months and as a result of their remarkable efforts, disruption to the normal running of school has been kept to a minimum. I must also praise our students for the manner in which they have coped with so much upheaval. What I can say definitely is that it was all worth it in the end".

On a personal note, as Chair of Governors, I would like to add my thanks and appreciation to these teams and particularly to Laura and Matthew Bennett and the rest of the catering team who worked in quite dreadful conditions, with no natural light, to provide the best possible service for our students.

At the end of November, Year 11 students sat their mock exams and Year 13 students sat them in January, all oblivious to the fact that there would be no external GCSEs or 'A' Level examinations in 2020 and life would be very different!

There were also some wonderful individual student achievements in November.

Mollie Wedgwood's dedication and commitment to Performing Arts throughout her years at Alsager School was rewarded with a place at the highly prestigious MetFilm School in London. MetFilm has an annual intake of 12 students per year, so only 'the best of the best' gain places.

Mollie has performed in every school play from year 7 to 13 playing a range of characters such as; Mayzie in Suessical, Mrs Sowerberry in Oliver, Rizzo in Grease and most recently Miss Hannigan in this year's production of Annie. Mollie is an immense talent and a fantastic ambassador for performing arts at Alsager School.

Chloe Brakner's essay won first prize in the humanities section of the Pembroke College, Oxford, essay-writing competition and recently visited the College to collect her certificate. As a Psychology 'A' level student, she entered her 2500 word essay responding to the question 'Is Society in Moral Decline'?

Christ Church hosted the second of the school's award ceremonies on 11th December when the class of 2019 celebrated their exceptional GCSE and BTEC successes. Alongside students receiving their GCSE certificates, a variety of special awards were presented to students who had shown exemplary determination throughout their journey at Alsager School. Students who made the most progress, demonstrated fortitude within their subjects and accomplished remarkable successes during their time at school were particularly commended for their achievements. The class of 2019 was an outstanding year group who responded fantastically to the challenges of GCSE examinations. One of the guest speakers was Dr Gavin Hammond, current Physics teacher and former student, who spoke about his inspiring journey through education and his work in a variety of fields. His words were rousing and showed students that with resilience and a lifelong love of learning, young people can accomplish great things.

Finally in December Mrs Ellen Walton, our Deputy Head, was appointed Headteacher at Sandbach Girls School and Sixth Form College. An amazing achievement. Ellen's dedication and drive are second to none and I can only describe her as 'a force of nature'. Sandbach will never be the same again! Of course, I say that with the most positive of sentiments and wish her every success in her new post.

It was in January 2020 that I learned that the new Sixth Form College building was to be called 'The Purcell Building'. It was a proud moment for me and my family. I was deeply honoured and delighted to have this wonderful, new facility named after me. Alsager School has always been a very special place to study and work, full of delightful young students and dedicated, talented staff.

I found Mr Middlebrook's comments, at the naming ceremony, very emotional and had to scan the gathering at one point, to see if he was really talking about me.

"Lindsay's passion, loyalty and commitment to Alsager School is quite exceptional. He is part of the fabric of the school so it is fitting that we now have the 'Purcell Building'. Lindsay cares passionately about this school and the people (past and present) who have worked and studied here. Everyone associated with Alsager respects him and I would personally like to thank him for everything he has done for our school."

Also In January, the Alsager School's Competition Choir sailed

Lindsay Purcell with students and the Purcell Building name plate.

through the first round of the Love Music Trust's 'Choir of the Year.' competition. Our ultra-talented and hard-working choir won the heat and thought they were on the way to yet another final. We have won this competition three times in the last four years, including last year...so the pressure was on to defend the title!

From 26th to 28th February, the annual school production, 'Annie', was performed over three nights to packed audiences. There were also two matinee performances for local primary schools. It was a delightful, colourful, extravaganza which celebrated the collaboration between the Music, Drama, Dance and Art departments, as well as incorporating pupils from Cranberry, Excalibur, Highfields, Pikemere and Weston primary schools. Mr Galley, Subject Leader of Music, said:

"Over 150 students and staff from within the Alsager community worked together as a team to produce a brilliant show and it was marvellous to be part of that team. I would just like to say how fantastic our students were this year. From the back stage team,

lights, sound and pit band, through to the chorus, dancers, main cast and all 5 primary schools. I was simply blown away by their commitment, enthusiasm and performance standards. We hope they all enjoyed the journey from the rehearsal stages to the performances themselves".

For my part, I would just like to say that I have watched Alsager School productions over many years and Annie was as good, if not better, than any I have ever seen. I left the Hollinshead Hall enthralled with the quality of the performance. A friend in the audience, who had taken her children to the Regent Theatre to see Annie last year, thought the Alsager School production was superior.

To date, this had been an academic year to savour with so many positive outcomes for the school. However, the world was beginning to learn about strange happenings in a previously unheard of city in China. The World Health Organisation began expressing concern about a new virus and on 11th February, it was named 'Covid 19'. On 11th March, the WHO declared Pandemic status and on 18th March Secretary of State for Education, Gavin Williamson ordered schools to close on 20th March. He defended his decision by saying:

"I've said before that if the science and the advice changed, such that keeping schools open would no longer be in the interests of children and teachers, then we would act".

Having closed its doors to all pupils on 20th March, Alsager School re-opened for vulnerable children and the children of key workers on March 23rd and remained open throughout the period of 'lockdown'.

The teaching profession suffered from a good deal of ill-informed commentary in the tabloid press during this period. However, at Alsager School, an enormous amount of work was going on behind the scenes, to interpret Government guidelines and plan for future eventualities, which were prone to frequent change. Remember in those early days, we were 'following the science' and the nation waited with 'baited breath' each afternoon, for Matt Hancock's latest pronouncement (or was it 'fake news'?)

Meanwhile, back at school, preparations were being made to adjust the fabric of the school according to health and safety regulations. Risk assessment policies were being adapted in preparation for the return of students, whenever that might be and those students who were in school had to be cared for and taught, so staffing rotas had to be prepared.

It did not stop there. Communication with all teaching staff had to be immediate and on-going as 'centre-assessed grades' had to be created as soon as it became apparent that there would be no external examinations in the Summer term of 2020. This presented a huge workload and responsibility for staff. Assessment protocols had to be written and rigorous moderation procedures established within curriculum areas and across the school. In short, an enormous logistical operation sprang to life.

Beyond the demands of external assessment, our students had to be taught. Years 12 and 10 were the highest priority because they were already in the external exam system. The Principles of Home Learning had to be quickly established, it could not be an ad-hoc system, left completely to the devices of the individual teacher. On-line communication systems had to be set up with all homes, teachers had to prepare schemes of work to take them through the lockdown period and monitoring systems had to be put into effect. These lessons were up and running very quickly but the school, after a few weeks, began to consider ways of varying practice.

Some staff had already experimented with 'live lessons' and this seemed the way forward - to bring the classroom to the home. Instruction files were e-mailed out to students and Microsoft Teams became the order of the day. I am reliably informed that Alsager School was the first school in Cheshire East to deliver live lessons to students. A real 'feather in our cap' during such challenging times.

I also enjoyed looking at 'Alsager Still at Work' on the school website. This was an amazing platform for sharing news, stories, actions and photographs. There were many, many pieces of students' work I could have chosen from this but I chose just two, to illustrate the sort of creativity and interaction between student and teacher. The first is by a Year 7 student Ava Barnes who created a set for Shakespeare's Twelfth Night. As you can see a marvellous piece of improvisation.

Ava Barnes' work.

Evan Bowers - VE Celebrations.

The second piece of practical work is by Evan Bowers whose afternoon tea party for the VE Celebrations looked absolutely sumptuous.

Well done Ava and Evan.

On the subject of 'Going live with Teams', Governors followed suit and resumed their programme of meetings using this on-line platform. In my opinion, although not nearly as good as 'face to face' meetings, an effective substitute.

For me, as Governor and former parent, the most impressive aspect of our lockdown provision was the way in which the school tried its best to continue to care for the well-being of its young people, despite the lack of day to day, face to face contact. Communication was on a regular basis, with Form tutors contacting each student. I looked forward to reading Mrs O'Neil's weekly chats with students, encouraging them with so many meaningful, positive, quotes about life and sharing her innermost weaknesses, like her love of 'Big Macs'. On 1st June 2020 her message to all students read as follows:

"Good afternoon,

I hope that you are all well and have had an enjoyable week off. The weather has been lovely which always helps to lift the mood.

I know that many of you had your first virtual lesson today. I would love to hear from you about it, as I know many of you were a little nervous! I hope that it was nice to hear your teachers' voices.

There are now many things that we can start to do which I am sure you are all really pleased about. It is great that you can start to meet up with more people but you must make sure that you are sensible with this and still follow the guidelines. We have all done really well so far.

I am extremely excited about the premier league starting up. I was beginning to dread all the Man City fans saying that Liverpool had been 'handed' the title! I also heard a rumour that McDonald's Drive Thru is opening up soon. That is really good news. I am beginning to have dreams of a Big Mac, fries and a shake! You just can't beat it, can you?

There are many things that I have missed during lockdown, but I wonder what we will miss about lockdown itself? I imagine many of you have been able to find something positive about this time. I would love you to share that with me. I have enjoyed listening to the birds in the garden. Apparently because of the reduction in noise pollution, more birds are 'talking' to each other! I recommend sitting outside and tuning in. It is very entertaining.

So as we enter a very bizarre final half term, I want you all to strive to do your best and remember, if things get tough, dig deep".

"The capacity to learn is a gift; the ability to learn is a skill; the willingness to learn is a choice" - (Brian Herbert, author).

The College Managers and SEND Team, led by Adele Snape, also did so much to stay in contact with our most vulnerable children, to ensure that they were continuing to stay safe and engaging with school life.

Finally, of course, there were the staff who also needed 'tender loving care' during this difficult period. Their world had changed too and it was important that the SLT kept their emotional needs firmly in mind.

On 15th June, Year 10 returned to school. It was by no means a normal school experience for them but it was a start! They were taught English, Maths and Science, in their Science sets, and each group returned for one morning per week. Attendance was amazing, which showed how much young people missed school and their friends. All the social distancing and hygiene regulations were adhered to incredibly well by our students.

Year 12 returned on 26th June, with equally impressive results and each Year 7 form spent a day in school, the week beginning 7th July.

I would like to end this chapter on 'A Year Like No Other' with two poems. One by by Sam Pickering who at the time was in Year 7 and one by Year 7LTa Form Tutor, Ms Taylor.

Lockdown Learning

I used to be quite happy,
I used to go to school.
But then we had to lock our doors,
That was a horrid rule.

The dreaded night that I found out,
That school would have to close.

I went and shut and locked my room,
And found it hard to doze.

So on the dawn of the next day,
I rushed around for books.
The teachers were the greatest help,
They gave me some textbooks

On Monday it was clear,
I wasn't going to learn
As much as I had done at school.
It made my stomach churn.

But even then the teachers found
A super way to teach.
They managed to get some work to us,
Until we're back in reach.

Maths could send my sums to me,
And then I wrote a tale
And sent it back to English,
Using our school e-mail.

But even that was not enough,
To make it just the same.
The school then made another way,
Into our homes they came.

They called them our "Live Lessons",
With Skype or using Teams,
I call this "Ingenious!"
It sewed the missing seams.

So here we are at present day,
Where I am happier.
Which only leaves me with one thing,
There's one last barrier.

I cannot go to see my friends,
I cannot see their face.
I just want to be back at school,
Cause that's my favourite place.

Sam Pickering (Year 7)

Lockdown Learning indeed! Well done Sam, I think you've summed up the feelings of many of your fellow students wonderfully well and need to be congratulated for the way in which you have encapsulated your thoughts in verse. As a Governor and former teacher at Alsager School, I was delighted to read it's your *"favourite place"*. You will go far in this world!

Equally, Ms Taylor captured beautifully the bond that exists between herself and her form in the poem below. If anything reflects 'the caring school' claim in the school's mission or the work on school culture that has been going on over the last year, it is this poem. Congratulations Ms Taylor.

Miss Taylor's Form, 7LTa appears above at the Kingswood Centre.

Dear 7LTa,

I wanted to thank you for giving me the most wonderful first year at Alsager School. I am so happy that I got to spend a day with you before the end of term. You were fantastic!

You continue to make me so proud. The way in which you have risen to the challenges of lockdown is testament to your character and determination. You are kind, you are compassionate, and you are strong.

Here is a reflection on our first year together:

September seems some time ago,

And just as we found our form time flow,

Covid-19 arrived and mixed things up,

I'm scared there'll now be mould in my cup!

We had the very best start to the term,

I'm always kind, but sometimes I'm firm!

But it serves us all very well,

Our BfLs are always swell!

Every week I feel so very proud,

When I read all our achievements out loud,

Big Breakfasts, free lunches and sporting wins,

Rare BfL 3s are our only sins!

What I admire about you all,

Is that if you experience a trip or fall,

You jump back up, you dust yourself down,

With a smile on your face and rarely a frown.

You're kind to each other, you hold open the door,

You're fun and you tear up the TikTok dancefloor,

You care for each other, the rules you don't flout,

We've had the best year, without a doubt.

Who predicted that all of this would occur?

It happened so fast, it seems such a blur!

On the 20th of March the schools would close,

But you're resilient and strong - to the challenge you rose!

Your emails inspired me and kept a smile on my face,

You've acted with such integrity and grace,

I've loved seeing pictures of what you have done,

You've worked so hard, you've also had fun.

You created volcanoes,

Baked cakes for Pride,

You walked in nature

and went for bike rides.

So much has happened whilst we were apart,

Overwhelming at times, especially the start,

You showed tolerance when the world seemed unkind,

You listened, you learned, you expanded your mind.

You took this time, you chose to grow,

You participated in lessons to show what you know,

You stayed so strong and showed self-regulation,

I missed seeing your faces in registration.

It must have been tempting to want to give in,

But you dug deep, you experienced the win,

Your commitment to learning never did sway,

You know very well 'that's the Alsager way!'

Chapter 14: What does the future hold for Alsager School?

All schools are facing challenging times. A look into Alsager School's future reveals a number of pressing issues, most notably its ability to balance its budget. In real terms there may be further reductions in the Education Services Grant, which funds academies. This problem is compounded by local funding issues i.e. the fact that Cheshire East is one of the most poorly funded Local Authorities in England and the LA's refusal to implement the National Funding Formula. School expansion will 'cost' the school for the next four years, as funding for the extra students on roll is retrospective and has to be covered by the school, with very little extra support. Increased national insurance and pension contributions for teaching and support staff and cost of living pay rises for all staff, which often are passed onto schools, are a continual drain on the budget. Perhaps the greatest budgetary challenge of all is uncertainty about government intentions.

With all the new building in Alsager, managing the growth of the school will present further challenges for staff and strains on resources and space. Equally, developing the Multi Academy Trust and supporting other schools, while maintaining highest possible standards at Alsager School, will mean that senior leaders and governors must ensure adequate capacity and not take their 'eyes off the ball'.

Teacher recruitment and retention will always be an issue, particularly in certain curriculum areas, where there are significant shortages already. Over the years Alsager School has been very fortunate to have been able to recruit high quality specialist teachers, but it always needs to be mindful of future teacher supply markets.

Another challenge will be striking the correct balance between motivating and inspiring our young people but not exerting pressures to the point that some opt out and struggle with mental health issues. To this end the school has recently received the prestigious AcSeed accreditation, for its work in fostering well-being and resilience amongst its students.

Also, it seems that Covid-19 is going to be with us for quite some time and will challenge even the most imaginative strategic thinkers, on how best to create the 'new normal' in their schools.

And now for the good news! There are so many positive developments going on at Alsager School and a great many possible ways forward. Just as Tony Blair set out his priority for his second term of office as Education, Education, Education, I would set a priority of Collaboration, Collaboration, Collaboration. In this way, schools can share ideas, expertise and best practice. They can share and centralise support functions to avoid duplication and enjoy economies of scale. Finally, they will have enhanced power as collective units, working together for the greater good.
There are already excellent examples of collaboration working effectively through the Chimney House Partnership of secondary schools in Cheshire East, Alsager Community Trust and of course Alsager Multi Academy Trust. Long may these organisations continue to be a force for improving the quality of teaching and learning in our locality.

Thankfully, there is now some evidence that schools are being judged on a broader range of outcomes than simply examination success and this is reflected in the latest OFSTED framework and some of the press releases from Amanda Spielman, the head of that organisation. A number of years ago, I came across a quote from a Randi Weingarten who was president of the American Federation of Teachers and Educationists. He said:

"Standardised testing is at cross purposes with many of the most important purposes of education. It doesn't measure big picture learning, critical thinking, perseverance, problem solving, creativity or curiosity, yet those are the qualities great teaching brings out in a student".

While I believe that external examinations and standardised testing do have a necessary part to play in the British education system, we ignore 'big picture learning', and those other aspects from Mr Weingarten's statement, at our peril.

Alsager School is an outstanding school. The quality of teaching is admirable. In spite of the pressures, teachers still find time to teach in incredibly imaginative ways, which stimulate and engage young people. All of this would not be possible without the huge network of superb support staff, to whom I am eternally grateful. I am filled with confidence for the future of my eldest grandchild as she moves into the secondary phase of her education at this school.

Throughout my long association with the School, it was always a great pleasure working with so many talented and dedicated staff. Reflecting back on how many of their lives unfolded, there may be some validity in dividing them into two groups. Firstly, those staff, like myself, who committed their careers to the school, over a great many years, for whatever reason. Secondly, those who used the school as a 'spring board', often to go on and achieve great things, within the education sphere and beyond. I can think of no better training ground for a young person to grow and develop, before moving on in pursuit of their careers. Many of these people are still in contact with the school and their particular mentors and friends, whose advice and guidance they will value for ever. Staff support and development of expertise are a major strength of the school and something we should all be proud of.

Finally, to the young people (and not so young any more), of Alsager School, it has always been a pleasure teaching you and being part of your school community. I apologise once again if your name does not appear in this book. I wish you all good health and happiness in your lives.

Lindsay Purcell

Appendices

Appendix One

Learning Assessment Results

1. Six
2. 1971
3. Margaret Thatcher
4. 22
5. Four - Margaret Thatcher, Sir Keith Joseph, (the longest serving secretary with 5 years) David Blunkett, Michael Gove
6. 1993
7. Mrs Val Hollins (38 years), Mr Steve Marshall (37), Mr Mike Elkin (36), Mrs Joyce Halsall (36), Mr Alvan Ikoku (36), Mr Gavin Gallimore (36) Ms Sonia Cross (35).
8. 1988
9. PE and RE
10. Tony Blair
11. Four
12. 2016
13. Seven
14. 2013 - Greater autonomy over budget and where money is allocated e.g. salaries, curriculum. MATs benefit from economies of scale and shared staffing and expertise.
15. Alsager Community Trust - the partnership of all Alsager Schools

Appendix Two

Staffing

Alsager School Executive Headteacher (New position in 2018)
Richard Middlebrook

Alsager School Headteachers
John Hughes
Austin Hawkes
Frederick Parker
Jim Andrews
David Black
Richard Middlebrook

Alsager School - Head of School (New position in 2019)
Andrea O'Neill

Deputy Headteachers
Miss Win Holmes
John King
Sheila Riley
Ian Macpherson
Jim Edwards
Philip Clarke
Hedley Austen
Lindsay Purcell
Jill Bristow
Keith Plant
Sonia Cross
Andrea O'Neill
Ellen Walton
Liane Young
Adele Snape

Assistant Headteachers

Jill Bristow
Keith Plant
Mel Smith
Dave Pointon
Sonia Cross
Chris Usher
Katie Phelan (Cochrane)
Andrea O'Neill
Heidi Thurland
Ellen Walton
Neil Williams
Liane Young
Adele Snape
Lianne Jardine
Rob Pearce

Heads of Year/Senior Tutors

Mike Elkin
Eric Marshall
Diane Heath
Mair Needham
Graham Harvey
Shirley Cross
Val Hollins
Jan Shaw
Christine Routs
Norman Boughey
Pat Sutton
Brenda Steele (Thomas)
Carol See
Janet Wells

Sixth Form

Reverend John Hughes
Keith Plant
Jackie Latham

Joanne Williams
Andrew Wishart
Alison Pole
Andrew Evans

College Managers
Brenda Steel (Thomas)
Janet Wells
Caryn Rawlins
Melanie Parker
Stewart Clegg
Jenny Broad
Nicola Gamwell
Gill Potts

The 35 Year Club (staff who have worked at the school 35 years or longer)
Mavis Broad 45 years+
Val Hollins 38 years
Steve Marshall 37 years
Alvan Ikoku 36 years
Mike Elkin 36 years
Joyce Halsall 36 years
Gavin Gallimore 36 years
Sonia Cross 35 years

The 25 Year Club (Staff who have worked at school 25 years or longer)
Miriam Clarke, Alan Danby, Keith Plant, Hilda Howard, Peter Lloyd, John Lyne, Norman Boughey, Jeff Halsall, Lindsay Purcell, Hazel Ash, Graham Harvey, Medwyn Jones, George Bull, Douglas Barnett, Brenda Steel (Thomas), Graham Lee, Graham Marsden, Margaret Jackson, Dennis Jackson, Heather Pitts, Mair Needham, Mel Smith, Trevor Sparrow, Philip Horsham, Trevor Worsley, Andy Pennance, Chris Metcalf, Annette Owen, Andrew Evans, Jackie Latham, Pat Arnott.

Bibliography

Alsager Multi-Academy Trust: An Overview of AMAT, December 2016

Alsager School Headteacher Log Books, 3 Volumes, 1955-2020.

Alsager School Newsletter: 'Headlines', 1992-2005.

Alsager School Newsletter: 'School Matters', 2006-2017.

Alsager School Newsletter: 'The Alsager SPIRIT', 2018-2020.

Castle F. and Evans J. 'Specialist Schools- What do we know?', A report by RISE, Research and Information on State Education, 2006.

Cullen, Dr J., 'So what is a MAT?' Open Learn, Open University Free Learning, 2018.

Department for Education Guidance Document, The EBacc, June 2015, updated August 2019.

Department for Education Pamphlet, 'Keeping Children Safe in Education', Information for all School and College Staff, September 2019.

DfES, NAHT, SHA, NASUWT et al. Report, 'Raising Standards and Teaching Workload: a National Agreement, January 2003.

Gee R. and Jarrett R. 'I'm a designated Safeguarding Governor ...Get me out of here!!' Cheshire East Governor Training Notes, 2018. Government Policy Green Paper, 'Every Child Matters' September 2003.

LinkedIn Professional Profiles, 2020

Lipinski D.G. 'What does it mean to be an Academy School?' BBC Family and Education News, May 2016.

Manchester Evening News, 'Leader in his Field', 19th April 2010.

National College for Teaching and Leadership: Leading and Developing Staff, Section 5 Teacher Appraisal, 2020

OFSTED, Alsager School Reports, February 2013 and February 2016

Purcell L., 'Planning for Contraction: A Case Study of Alsager School', MSc. Dissertation, 1985.

Sutton J.C. MA. Editor, 'Alsager the Place and its People', Alsager History Research Group, 1989.

The Key for School Governors - Sections relating to Academies and MATs; Staff Pay, Appraisal and Development; Safeguarding and the Governing Body, 2020.

Weston D. and Campbell I., 'Transforming Teacher Performance is within easy reach', Schools Weekly, August 2020.

Welsh National Opera, Claire Hampton Profile, 2020.

Wikimedia Foundation, Wikipedia online encyclopaedia career profiles, 2020.

"Only look back at life's work well done and fond memories of family and friends"

L Purcell, 2020